Six Sigma -
Understanding the Concept, Implications and Challenges

Other books by Mario Perez-Wilson

Multi-vari Chart and Analysis - A Pre-experimentation Technique-

Positrol Plans and Logs - A Plan for Controlling Variation during
Production -

Six Sigma -
Understanding the Concept, Implications and Challenges

by Mario Perez-Wilson

For books,
public seminars,
in-house training seminars, and
consulting services

Call

Advanced Systems Consultants
Post Office Box 1176
Scottsdale, Arizona 85252-1176
U.S.A.
Phone (480) 423-0081
Fax (480) 423-8217
Email: asc@mpcps.com
WebPage: www.mpcps.com

To Jaclyn with all my love.

Acknowledgements

The author would like to offer his special thanks to the following individuals:

Manuel Barua, for his encouragement in writing and sharing the anecdotes that brought us so many laughs. Sorry I had to stop at 1987. Time caught up with me.

Manuel Figueroa, for his critical reading and editing of the manuscript.

Jaclyn Perez-Wilson, my wife, for her patience, understanding and encouragement.

Copyrights

Cover Designed by:
Visual Media Arts
13132 North 22nd Avenue,
Phoenix, Arizona 85029
Tel: 602-942-5957
visualmedia@speedchoice.com

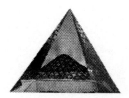

Crystal designed by:
Jan Stohanzl, Prague, Czech Republic
Copyright, 1998 Jan Stohanzl

The original manuscript was
pleasurely hand written with a
MontBlanc Meisterstuck - Agatha
Christie - Limited Edition
Fountain Pen #08626

Contents

Part I
Six Sigma - A Novel

Part II
Six Sigma, the Concept, Implications and Challenges

Introduction

Understanding Six Sigma

The M/PCpS Methodology to Achieve
Six Sigma

Appendix

Preface

Recently, the concept of Six Sigma has catapulted back to the forefront of many a quality professional's interest in a growing number of organizations. Unfortunately, it has been elevated to almost mythological heights by cure-all claims made both by industry leaders and the myriad consultants who are now jumping into the Six Sigma bandwagon. Instead of clarity and understanding, the clamor of these born-again cheerleaders seems to be muddying the waters, adding confusion to an already misunderstood subject.

Six Sigma is about treating most operations as systems and about improving the processes that occur within those systems. It is about reducing process variation and about reducing the value of the sigma (the standard deviation), so as to fit twelve standard deviations within the specification limits. Six Sigma is NOT about having the process average shift ±1.5 sigmas and it is NOT about producing defects, errors or mistakes at a 3.4 ppm level. On the contrary, it is about NOT having the process average shift at all and about producing defects, errors or mistakes at a mere 0.002 ppm level - for all practical purposes, it is about reducing defects, errors and mistakes to virtually zero.

No doubt, Six Sigma attempts to provide a scientific approach and discipline to the practice or pursuit of process improvement and can seem quite technical. Nevertheless, in this book, I have made a serious effort to explain the concept of Six Sigma in a fashion that I hope will be understood by most everybody, not just by technical people. As consultants, we often find ourselves in the role of teachers; and, as teachers, we have the duty to use our expertise to simplify matters and put in an extra effort to explain them in a fashion that serves our students - or our customers - well.

During a visit to the Czech Republic, I was able to witness the production of artifacts in lead crystal, an art the Czech people have mastered and passed along from generation to generation.

The pyramid crystal in the cover page is the personification of Six Sigma. The pyramid represents the robust approach to excellence embraced by Six Sigma. The crystal represents the clear philosophical vision of Six Sigma. And the 3-D bell-shaped curve represents the Normal distribution, the statistical foundation of Six Sigma.

The first part of the book is a novel, told in a series of vignettes. I suggest you read it carefully because, intertwined within the narrative of each vignette, you will find much useful and practical information about Six Sigma. I prefer not to make any further comments; I just hope you find it interesting, enlightening and somewhat entertaining.

The second part of the book is my serious attempt at demystifying and clarifying Six Sigma. I have tried to provide a clear, layman's explanation of what it is and how it can be achieved. It is a subject well-worth understanding because Six Sigma can provide a crystal clear vision and a robust structure to bring about change and excellence in an organization.

I've also included a Glossary and an Index, which I hope you find useful, and a section that answers most of the questions I have been receiving in Emails. In the spirit of this new and exciting age of information prompted by the Internet, this section is appropriately entitled "Frequently Asked Questions" or FAQs. If after reading the book you still have questions about Six Sigma, please write to me at the address on the next to last page of the book and I'll try to further clarify the subject and answer your questions.

Mario Perez-Wilson
Prague, Czech Republic
May 6th, 1998

Part I

Six Sigma
- A Novel -

Life Before Six Sigma

"Definitely, I don't know how they do it. For the last three days the yield on that wave solder machine has been at its lowest level and nobody in my department can tell me how to fix it or what the hell went wrong." Harry, the Manufacturing Manager, spoke loud, proud and with a heavy Texan accent.

Well, he had a good reason for it: he was brought into the program from the facility in Texas, which had a reputation for doing things right. But somehow, the glow of efficiency and innovation wasn't coming from his department. It was coming from the quality department, which Harry considered more of a thorn in his side than a source of support.

Harry held his early meeting in his own office and all the manufacturing engineers had to stuff themselves in the little room, like sardines. "We're reworking every damn circuit board', we have over 180 defects per board, and the customer is making a special trip to come and see us. Meanwhile, all you guys can tell me is he has shown you a few boards that look beautiful with but maybe one or two defects. How in the hell can he do that when you guys have been working for the last three days and you keep on telling me it's the board supplier?" complained Harry.

"Well, Sir, apparently he and his team stayed after five and worked all night running an experiment, " answered Fred.

"Well, how can they do that? The machine is ours, the process is ours, the parts are ours! How did they get past us? Who gave them permission to mess with our equipment?" asked Harry.

"Well, Sir, Ned, the Production Supervisor; he stayed with them all night," said Fred hesitantly,

"Why do I have to be surprised with these things? Ned reports to me. How come Ned didn't inform me? I want you to call him now. I want him in my office, now!" said Harry raising his voice.

"Well, Sir, Ned wanted to learn how they have been figuring out how to set up the processes, and decided to stay with them the whole night; and by the way, he left this note on my desk."

"What does it say?" asked Harry quickly, without even letting him finish the sentence.

"It says they have figured it out; a new setup that works just beautiful. No major changes and using the same boards. The boards come out almost perfect. Oh yeah, it also says he will be in late, around noon."

Harry was furious. This was not the first time this had happened. It was starting to be a little game: every time the yield in one of the operations went down and the defect levels increased, this engineer - Mario - from the quality department would conduct a little brainstorming session with his own private team, come after working hours (the process ran in only one shift) and run an experiment.

Harry didn't know it but, afterwards, Mario and his team would finish the analysis and contemplate the data at the Salt Cellar Restaurant while drinking a few beers; and then go home, sleep but a few hours, and come in early to produce a report with the findings.

The little game was starting to piss off more than just Harry; a few manufacturing engineers were starting to look like fools. The production operators and the quality inspectors, on the other hand, were loving every minute of it; to them it was like having their own Robin Hood.

After all, the operators were the ones that suffered the most from these process shut downs. They were the ones who had to come on the weekend to run more product to meet quotas. Nothing frustrated them more than having a manufacturing engineer who was not able to fix a process, or give them a straight answer about what was wrong. And when they, the operators, suggested an idea on how to possibly correct the problem, the manufacturing engineers wouldn't even consider or try the operators' idea. The engineers would immediately discard the idea with the statement, "That won't work!"

"Fred," said Harry, "I want you to bring Mario to my office. Let's see if we can prevent him from publishing another memo."

The "memo" consisted of a report and a cover memo. Unknown to Harry at the time, the "memo" had already been written and sent for distribution. It showed specifically all the experimental combinations Mario and his team had tested, along with all the analysis and conclusive evidence. And, as usual, Mario's report also showed the "significant difference" in the reduction of defects and specified the process parameters which would guarantee beautiful results from the process.

Nothing was more upsetting to Harry than the smooth flow and the logical progression in the investigatory and exploratory analysis described in those reports. No stone was left unturned; all the possibilities had been explored and all the steps justified. The objective was always correlated with the conclusions and the recommendations; and the course of action was spelled out in layman's terms, for anybody to understand or rebut. Those reports were like a compass.

Maybe what upset Harry the most was the fact none of his manufacturing engineers had those skills; and not one had a clear direction in root-cause problem-solving. And, although

Harry mastered the lingo of statistical process control and preached SPC to his engineers, it was evident it was only lip service. His mantra was: "Don't stop my process and don't tell me we're producing defective product; and, if quality assurance tells us our products are coming out defective, wait for us to contain and then fix the problem at our own pace."

Fred walked to Mario's cubicle and said, "You've done it again. Harry wants you in his office, now!"

Harry's office was not too far away, but whenever he was called in, Mario felt like it was miles away and his whole career flashed through his head in a matter of seconds.

Most people in the program, at one point or another, had either been witness to, or heard the rumors of Harry's screaming and eating someone alive, and not just his subordinates but, on a few occasions, his colleagues. With that karma, nobody wanted to be on his bad side.

Somehow, the office felt crowded, but it was only the two of them there. Harry's commanding presence just filled the room and Mario felt, like most people, as if Harry were breathing down his neck - not a pretty picture. Most people, when called in, would just talk to him from the door, without stepping in; it gave them a feeling of security.

Mario entered Harry's office. "Good morning, Harry, how are you today? What can I do for you?"

"Fred mentioned you ran an experiment last night and

the boards looked pretty good. We have a customer meeting this afternoon and I need to show them we're implementing SPC; this would be a perfect opportunity to show them the result," Harry said nonchalantly.

"Well, Harry, I'm finishing the last touches on my report and it should be out before your meeting," Mario shot back. He was not about to simply give him the boards and the results and let him take credit for it.   He wanted to ensure it was all formally documented.

"The bureaucracy around here is just pathetic!" Harry snorted. "Why the hell do we have to wait and go through delays by writing reports and memos? In the commercial side of this company, we operate informally and we make changes faster than in this Government program."

"Well, Harry, I am proposing changes in the wave solder parameters that could significantly reduce solder defects. This is not just my opinion. I have data that proves it with a high confidence level. So, as you can see, I have to put this in writing."

"Well, Mario, if you just give me your proposed wave solder parameters, I'll just have my engineers confirm them."

"You want your engineers to confirm my results! Look, Harry, for the last three months I've been working on characterizing the whole process of the Fuze. I've put together a comprehensive plan to study each operation and equipment, and set a time table, but you haven't supported the program or lent any of your process engineers to the effort."

Just as Harry was about to say something, Mario continued, "And furthermore, you criticize the whole effort as a waste of time and claim the processes are already capable. Meanwhile, your engineers tell me they cannot help on the effort because you have a different priority. The yields on these so-called capable processes vary from 20 to 80 percent during a single week and every week it's a different problem; and these are the same problems they said they fixed three months ago!"

"Of course I support the efforts," said Harry, "but I have my engineers busy fixing problems all day long and they don't have time to concentrate their efforts on a single operation."

"Did you say support? The last time your people showed any interest was in the characterization of the Pin Inserter, and they only studied one single response variable out of the four we had identified in the characterization plan for that operation. All they did was to study that one variable and they claimed victory when they fixed it. They said the other three variables were okay without even collecting data. I guess they're gifted with that engineering skill of learning by osmosis. But, now they're probably busy fixing problems associated with those three responses they overlooked," Mario said sarcastically.

"I need those results now! I have to show the customer we're making improvements. Are you going to give them to me or not?" Harry demanded.

"Rob mentioned he was going to present the findings on the Wave Solder experiment to the customer this afternoon. He was pretty impressed with the 98 percent increase in yield - and this is with our existing board supplier," said Mario.

Rob was the Quality Assurance and Program Manager and Mario's supervisor. He didn't like anybody rocking the boat, but he didn't mind presenting good results.

"But to answer your question: check your in-basket, there should be a memo describing the experiment. I wrote it last night; it should already be there by now. I'm still finishing the report. And by the way, the purpose of the report is to document and broadcast the use of statistical methods throughout the organization; so we can stop spreading tribal knowledge and have the engineers figure out the science of running these processes," Mario said as he turned to leave Harry's office.

——————— • ———————

Trying to implement statistical methods for the improvement of processes in an organization from the bottom up is virtually impossible, if not the most frustrating job.

——————— • ———————

What's the Difference Between Tree Rings and Bomb Fuzes?

For many years, the Tactical Division had the benefit of enjoying Merv, an exceptional PhD Statistician, on their staff. He had worked there for many years and all of his contributions were of outstanding quality and remarkable professionalism. He was also very well-liked and respected by his peers and colleagues. But in 1985, the unfortunate happened and Merv passed away. The Tactical Division - which was starting a new Fuze program with a phenomenal potential for high volume business - was left with no high caliber individual to implement statistical process control in the program from its infancy. After months of searching internally, the grapevine offered a possibility and a call was placed to an engineer from outside the Division.

Mario's years of working with the Laboratory of Tree-ring Research under the direct supervision of Dr. Harold Fritts - an authority in Tree-ring Research and Dendrochronology - had prepared him well to serve in a position that required implementing statistical methods in the real world. In the past, his application of statistics had been focused towards the reconstruction of past climates through the analysis of tree-ring data coming from all parts of the world. This time, the scope was different and his degree and added experience as an engineer would serve him well in this future endeavor.

Without literally applying for the position, Mario was surprised by a call for an interview. The interview didn't last long. They had carefully reviewed Mario's background without him knowing it; and, although the program was not classified, they had the means of knowing more than he was ever willing to tell.

The challenges of the position were very clear, concise and direct. First and foremost, they wanted somebody who would be professionally respected by his peers. At no time could the applicant lose credibility with his colleagues or the customer (in this case, the US Government: Navy, Air Force, China Lake, etc.) because, at the end of the day, they were not making candy, but High Explosive Bomb Fuzes which were expected to function perfectly - only once, the first time around.

The machines, tooling and equipment were already ordered and ready for delivery, and they wanted the program to be automatically controlled by statistical process control, SPC. This was going to be the first government program that, from its infancy, was going to use statistics in all the quality decision-making.

The plan was simple: identify the critical characteristics, set control charts at key locations in the production process and monitor the quality during production. If the control charts exhibited an out-of-control condition, correct the problem. Well, not so simple if the people who had to fix the problem were in denial and thought the problem was the data and not the process from which the data came. Of course, Mario didn't know this.

In the past, Mario's work at the Tree-ring Lab had been around scientists and researchers, and they were a breed apart; they were accustomed to collecting and analyzing data before making decisions. He was soon to discover his new group of colleagues were another breed, as well - first they made the decisions, then they collected the data to prove themselves. right!

So, full of enthusiasm for the new challenge, but concerned about taking the position of a deceased person, Mario decided to take the job. At the end of the day, he figured, what would be the difference between analyzing tree-ring data versus bomb fuze data? He would soon discover the significant difference.

_____ • _____

Implementing statistical methods in different products, processes, industries or subjects may not be the major

complication, the people and their level of acceptance and understanding of statistics may be the real stumbling block.

_____ • _____

The Little Game Cost Somebody's Job

Johnny was an old timer, not by age, but by time employed in the company. He was really fond of horses and his weekends were primarily spent with them. Every time a problem would potentially require extra work be extended into the weekend, he would say, "Don't freaking mess with my weekend!" He would do anything necessary during the week, just so his job would not touch his glorious weekend.

Johnny was in charge of the Spring Clip Insertion & Epoxy Curing process. The process had been running for quite awhile now and, as usual, it was being perfected as it was producing product - despite complains and insistence by a joint effort to characterize the process prior to production. But manufacturing wanted to follow their usual we fix it as we go along, even though the yield fluctuated between 20 and 80 percent from week-to-week and they produced more scrap than product. For some reason, that didn't matter; they felt like they were doing something.

It never occurred to them it was preferable to just stop the process, do experiments until a fix was found, and then proceed to run the process defect-free. Somehow, they preferred to tinker with it for long periods of time, fixing it many times throughout the months. Maybe they were doing it to justify their existence and employment; but probably, and more importantly, they also wanted to prove the process was something very complex and that it had too many variables.

For months, the Spring Clip Insertion & Epoxy Curing process was being redefined by Johnny, trying new changes and alterations without following any logical progression, just paying attention to the latest defects that were surfacing every week.

In one of the weekly problem days, epoxy was leaking into the unit, where the electronics were. This was definitely a major problem according to the customer print specifications.

The previous week, the spring-clips had not sat perpendicular against the end caps. To correct the problem, Johnny designed and ordered stainless steel lids that held the clips perpendicular to the end caps. These lids held the spring-clips in position during the epoxy curing operation inside an oven. The lids were designed and ordered with tolerances of ± 0.001 inch; very expensive requirements for the tooling vendor.

The stainless steel lids cost over $10,000 and Johnny had ordered 100 of them, enough to fill the whole oven. As usual, the change and solution to the new weekly problem went from idea, to design, to implementation; all without the proper risk or failure analysis, without properly testing and proving the solution to ensure it would bring significant improvements. And now, during implementation, the leakage was still present.

So, Johnny decided to focus now on changing the epoxy recipe. And every week it was the same crap: change this, change that. And the changes were no joke, either; they were expensive and they just demonstrated to the customer how little we knew of our processes.

Sick and tired of this modus operandi, Mario decided it was time to run another of the secretive overnight experiments. Calls were placed from the list of engineers who wanted to witness and possibly assist in the execution of an overnight experiment.

The word had been passed around among the engineers that, if you wanted to take part in running a real-life statistically-designed experiment with a real process, about the only place you could do that was in the Fuze program. Engineers in other programs were starting to get extremely interested in these efforts because they were not allowed to mess with their own processes. Many of them, frustrated with their nonsupportive management, decided to satisfy their learning curiosity by asking to be involved in the next experiment.

There were only three conditions for involvement in the

experiment: they would be informed on the same day the experiment was going to be executed; they would have to stay up all night, usually starting at 6:00 PM and going until 6:00 AM; and their time was pro-bono, they could not charge their time to the Fuze program.

The synergy these overnight experiments created was exceptional. Engineers from all different areas were calling in their requests to attend - including some of the current Six Sigma consultants now in business for themselves. Some would come from the Radar Division, others from the Communications Division and, regardless of their background, they were all interested in learning the applications of these experiments. More than anything, it was their chance to do something positive and proactive; an infusion of fresh blood to keep their soul alive in a lethargic routine of complacency.

Mario had proceeded with the program of Process Characterization with minimal support from manufacturing management. He had found some real support for the overnight experiments in those few adventurous engineers.

On the list was one bright engineer from the Radar Division, Barry (who now runs his own consulting firm). It was difficult to run experiments with the radar process because the resistance to change was even greater there, but he had heard about the Fuze program and was eager to be involved in planned experimentation.

As usual, the overnight team included the participation of Mark, the Production Quality Supervisor, who during his time off, would get involved in rodeo events, riding and roping steers - all true cowboy stuff. Mark was in charge of all the quality inspectors in the program and was always keen on applying statistical methods, but his current position didn't give him the opportunity to do so. Joining the overnight team was a way of satisfying his raging appetite.

The overnight experiment was set for the next night and it was going to include different oven conveyor speeds, temperatures, epoxy heights, and inclusion and exclusion of the stainless steel lids. In addition, the response characteristics were to include all customer print specification requirements to fix the process once and for all.

Vicky, the Quality Assurance Inspector Supervisor, who was always fun to have around, had joined the experiment team. Intelligent, witty and with a great personality, she enjoyed laughing hysterically at all the tales and stories the guys told her. Everybody in the team enjoyed her presence. She was certified in all the gauges and was going to inspect all the units coming out of the oven for all defects.

The experiment took about six full hours to run. It didn't take much analysis to figure out there were a few settings for the variables which would significantly improve the overall yield to very high levels. So, immediately, the team wanted to do a confirmation of the optimal conditions by running a bunch of units to make sure these new conditions could really impact the yield. Everybody was excited.

It's not often you can increase the yield with a first

experiment, but luck was on their side and they had combined the correct variables for this experiment. So immediately after the confirmation, they found themselves with a 100 percent defect-free product and with all other characteristics well within specifications.

The team had done good! They were all pumped up and nobody wanted the night to end. Everybody was making photocopies of all the data sheets and the results of the analysis, as if this were the prize for the night's work. They all assisted with the report and by 5:00 AM they were all in the parking lot, ready to go home with just enough time to take a quick shower and be back to work by 7:45 AM.

This time the results were so compelling that, by early morning, a report had already been left in everybody's in-basket. The impact would be felt immediately. But, on the other hand, the results were so overwhelmingly perfect they were going to make people very happy.

The only unhappy camper was going to be Harry, because he didn't approve of these overnight experiments - he felt they were making him look bad. But Mario knew this process tinkering Harry favored had to stop. And it was not going to be done by merely asking him to stop it, but by actually showing him and everybody else a new, better alternative approach.

By 8:00 that morning, most upper managers had read the report and were very pleased with the results. But, at the same time, all manufacturing engineers were already in Harry's office - packed like sardines, as usual - listening to Harry's loud, "Son-of-a-Bitch!" This time, he was beyond furious. He hated surprises and, especially, he hated anything coming from another department telling him his process was producing defective units or what he should do to correct it. He felt only they, the manufacturing department, should correct their process.

This time, Harry asked his senior engineer to take a few units and rerun the best conditions determined by the experiment, and to bring him the results ASAP. Then he asked all his staff to leave, with the exception of Johnny. He asked Johnny to show him the data to support the changes he had implemented. Johnny had none. Harry told him to get out!

By noon the results of the rerun were in and the yield was estimated to be at 100 percent. Not one single unit leaked with best settings and the perpendicularity of the spring clips were all within specification, and the stainless steel lids were not necessary; as a matter of fact, they were the cause of the leaks.

Apparently, the lids were placing a heavy mass on top of the end caps and holding the spring clips in position, but with little tolerance. As the units traveled on the conveyor belt through the oven, they vibrated and caused the epoxy to leak into the units' electronics. As soon as Harry saw the results, he called Johnny back to his office and fired him on the spot.

Rob, the Quality Assurance and Program Manager, was extremely excited the leakage problem had been put to rest. He was not interested in who had fixed the problem. He was solely interested in ensuring the program was ready to go into Full Scale Production (FSP) as soon as possible, without any major defects.

The program of Process Characterization was already designed, planned and scheduled for the Fuze program, but it was not being supported by manufacturing engineering.

As soon as Rob found out Johnny had been fired, and that $10,000 could have been saved had they followed up with the scheduled Process Characterization study, he decided to support the initiative full force. He wrote in the QA Plan that all pieces of equipment and all operations would have to undergo a Process Characterization study and, unless satisfactory results were obtained, the process would not be allowed to produce product and the equipment would be red-tagged and all inspection would cease.

This was the first and only time Rob stuck up for his people, but it had still cost somebody's job. It was a price Mario could not justify, so he ended the overnight experiments.

—————— • ——————

**The pursuit of the right thing to do,
and doing what is right, both yield their own rewards. But
often the price may be significant.
Change is not always easy or painless.**

—————— • ——————

It Takes Two to Tango

Rob, the Quality Assurance and Fuze Program Manager, felt the expulsion of Johnny was uncalled for and entirely a consequence of Harry's lack of commitment to the Process Characterization program. If the Process Characterization program had been supported from the very beginning, Johnny's faux pas would have never happened.

For starters, Johnny would have been well-trained and required to characterize, optimize and control his process before putting it into production. Somehow, he would have been persuaded to run some trials before ordering and wasting ten thousand dollars-worth of stainless steel lids. But given the program had not been supported by Harry, Johnny had had no chance of interfacing with people who could have advised him to run experiments.

Harry's real problem was the characterization program was not invented by him or by anybody else in his department. So, all he intended to do was give it lip service. He would not officially show his feelings against the program, because that would be corporate suicide. But, by not doing anything to encourage his people to support the program, he communicated quite clearly his true feeling and opinions.

Now, it was time for Rob to act, and so he did. He emphatically decided to finally support the program.

The Process Characterization program had already been very carefully designed, planned and scheduled, but it required the manufacturing engineers as well as the quality engineers becoming involved and working together. Some manufacturing engineers had been quite eager from the very beginning, but Harry had managed to constantly change their priorities; virtually eliminating any possibility of dedicating any time to the Process Characterization program. And this effort definitely required time and dedication to make it happen.

The program was cleverly simple. Every piece of equipment has a function, which is to modify a response or characteristic in the product - in this case, a fuze. The fuze has a customer print that specifies all the characteristics' specifications or tolerances. For the product to be perfect, it must have all its characteristics well within customer specifications. To ensure all its characteristics are always within specifications, requires a large sample of units be well-centered and clustered around the middle of the customer specification limits. So, all characteristics influenced by a machine or process are tested by surprising the process at a predetermined time. If a particular characteristic fails by having too much variability, then the process undergoes planned experimentation until it's optimized. Once all characteristics are well within print specifications, then, the Process Characterization program continues with the next machine in the schedule.

In layman's terms, the program means fixing everything that is not perfect until everything is fixed and the product is perfect. Once all machines, equipment and tools undergo a study like this, the whole process - in this case, comprising 35 pieces of equipment - is deemed capable of producing perfect product.

Discipline and focus are definitely major ingredients. Unfortunately, this discipline is not a virtue in people who have been brain-washed into just fire-fighting all through their careers, and who believe that's how they should be spending their time at work. Moreover, these were people whose college science education had taught them to test one thing at a time, while holding everything else constant. And here, in one single swoop, they were being asked to change many years of ingrained fix only what is broken, make a quick fix and change one factor at a time.

Rob called Mario to his office and asked him to close the door immediately. He was not the kind of boss who had closed-door meetings, so this was a clue that something was going on.

"I need to know, what I can do to make Harry support

your characterization program?" Rob asked.

"Well, how about having him report to me? Just kidding."

"Get serious," he said, not at all amused. "What would you like me to do?"

Rob had no sense of humor and was very respectful of the levels of authority. At no point would he even consider joking that rank should be broken. And he hated making waves. So asking for my input about Harry was a big deal to him - like breaking his code of honor.

"Well Rob," Mario said, "in that case, let me first tell you everything I've done, then we will figure out what we need to do to make this program work."

"Okay, go ahead Mario," he said.

"You know I identified every piece of equipment and operation on the production floor. And, I also identified the manufacturing engineer in charge of each of the operations. Each characteristic was also identified and I scheduled each study, giving them plenty of time to get them done."

"Yes, I'm aware of that. I saw your memo," Rob said. "As a matter of fact, Harry made a good comment about your memo."

"All the engineers were copied on this scheduled plan

and they all agree with it. Some came back to my cubicle and asked me to change and modify the schedule, but in the end, they all agreed," Mario continued.

"I'm aware of all that," Rob said, losing his patience.

"Well, once we started on the first study, we ran into a bunch of problems, and after that, the engineers were all upset and they didn't want to continue."

"So, what happened?" Rob asked.

"We decided to measure the first characteristic on the Lanyard Assembly operation and I asked the engineers if the gauge they were going to use was repeatable. And they told me, 'Of course it's repeatable; it's calibrated! Don't you see the calibration sticker? It is good until the 24th of November. It was calibrated a month ago.'" Mario elaborated.

"Okay, get to the point," said Rob, losing his patience again.

"Okay, so I told them I could see that, but what I meant was if the gauge was precise. They answered back, 'When we take the gauge to the central calibration department, what they do guarantees the gauge is good. What do you think? Do you think that if the gauge is no good, they would put a calibration sticker? Besides, we have to believe in something. If the gauge is calibrated, it's good for me. What the hell! Am I going to distrust everything now? You know, we trust our peers and their work. Next thing you're going to ask us is to measure every piece part that goes into this assembly to see if they're within specification limits, and we'll be here doing this all week, just to do one operation.'"

Mario could feel Rob's impatience, so he continued quickly, "So I decided to go on. 'Go ahead,' I told the engineers, 'measure the assemblies. Let's see what we get.' And they started to take the measurements. I told them we should run the equipment until we produced at least 30 assemblies. And immediately, they argued that it was only required to run about five, maximum ten. So I asked them where they got that idea. And one of them said, 'At the training seminar done by the PhD Statistician from the Communication Division, he took only five units on each experiment and that was all he needed, and he said more than ten readings would be too many.' Then another one said, 'So, if we take about ten that would be okay?' And the other manufacturing engineer agreed with him."

"So, they're obviously not understanding minimum sample sizes. That could be a problem," stated Rob.

"I know, so I decided to explain that for the standard deviation a large sample was needed. And the engineers just said, 'Let's just take the measurement and proceed.' They proceeded to measure a bunch of assemblies, which took them about half an hour. In many of the assemblies, the readings were all over the specification. They were not too happy about that and immediately they started making changes in the equipment. And we're not talking about one change, they made a whole bunch of changes all at once, before collecting any data."

"Wow," Rob said surprised.

"'So,' I asked them, 'from all of those changes you have just made, how are you going to know which change made an impact in improving the measurements in the assemblies? How could you tell which variable is responsible for an improvement when you change so many things at the same time?' So one of the engineers answered back, 'Well, before, I would have changed one thing at a time, holding everything else constant and measuring the assemblies. But in the seminar we were told that was a thing of the past, that now you run experiments where you change a number of variables at a time.'" Mario smiled waiting for Rob's reaction.

"What the hell are they teaching them in these seminars?" Rob exclaimed.

"I don't know Rob, but let me just finish telling you what happened," Mario said. "So, I told them, 'That only applies when you are running experiments and you have to do that in a controlled manner.' Now, here I was, discussing experimentation when in reality we were trying to characterize the process, not run experiments. We had not even finished collecting data to make an analysis on the first characteristic and these engineers wanted to run experiments with a process they didn't understand, gauges that were probably not repeatable, and using techniques which had them totally confused."

Now Rob was giving Mario his undivided attention. "Well, Rob," Mario said, "this felt like pissing against the wind; no matter what maneuvers you do, you're still going to get your shoes all wet!" Rob cracked a smile.

"So they decided to immediately run more assemblies," Mario continued. "Now they wanted to run only five and the variability was even worse than before. At this point, they were doing even more changes, and not only to one variable, they changed a whole lot of variables with no particular logic. No rhyme or reason. To the point the equipment could not even do one assembly correctly. Totally dysfunctional. At that point, I told them if they wanted to run an experiment, we should first plan it and design it before running it. They ignored me completely and continued to make adjustments. They were just too busy trying to make the equipment function properly again. After three hours of this random approach, they decided to setup the equipment as it was before."

Rob shook his head, "Go on."

"So, I decided maybe I should show them instead of telling them. And I said, 'We have here enough assemblies to do a repeatability study.' And I started taking various measurements with five assemblies. Then, I asked one of them to measure the same five assemblies. We proceeded like this a few times and then we computed the repeatability of the gauge. The number was huge as a percent of tolerance and it was obvious to them that for the same assembly, we were getting a spread of different readings. After fidgeting with the equipment for a bunch of hours and trying to tweak it, they finally realized the gauge had a problem."

Rob started to say something, but stopped, his mouth

half open.

Mario continued, "One of the engineers asked me, how come I had not shown them that from the very beginning. And I said, 'Well guys, you were just too busy making changes to the equipment.' So one manufacturing engineer concluded the gauge was the problem and the process was okay from the very beginning. 'Just because the gauge has some variability, that doesn't make your equipment devoid of all variability,' I said, 'We still have to submit your equipment to another study at a later time with a more repeatable gauge.' The gauge was sent to the central calibration department for recalibration. Now they're waiting for the gauge to come back."

Mario was getting a little edgy now. "Meanwhile," he continued, "they're placing the equipment back in production! There are four more characteristics in the Lanyard Assembly that require different gauges and they're proceeding to collect data without testing the repeatability of any of those gauges. In other words, they still believe the gauge had a problem and recalibrating it will fix its precision. They don't understand the basics! Calibration only deals with the accuracy of the gauges, it doesn't deal with precision and repeatability."

Rob looked down at his hands, but still said absolutely nothing.

"Now, Rob, all of these engineers have gone through the training presented by the PhD Statistician they have hidden in the other division, but obviously, they're coming from the training totally clueless as to how to apply these techniques.

They're more dangerous now, with the little knowledge they have gotten from these seminars. Now they even argue using the technical lingo, sounding more assertive and knowledge-able, despite their obvious ignorance. This internal consultant is teaching them the tools, but not the order in which they should be applied with a real manufacturing process."

"What are you trying to tell me?" interrupted Rob, sounding a bit upset.

"Well Rob, I would like to train them in how to use these tools and how to characterize a process."

Now Rob finally had something to say and he just couldn't hold it back anymore, "There is no way I will permit you to use your time retraining the manufacturing engineers! They would take that as an insult, and Harry would not go for that at all. He has already spent all his training budget for this year sending his engineers to that other training. They chose that PhD Statistician and we cannot tell Harry his engineers don't understand how to apply these tools. He would not sup-port the idea of you teaching them. He's already pissed at you because you ran your overnight experiments without his knowl-edge and without his engineers, and because you invited some people from the other division. By the way, I meant to ask you, who are these people?"

"Well, Rob, there's an audience out there. They're just a few engineers from other programs who want to assist and learn."

"Well, I don't condemn what you're doing with the overnight experiments - but I don't condone it, either. We have to get this program going into Full Scale Production defect-free, with either manufacturing fixing the problems or, in the worst case, you. But I don't want you to get all the heat. Harry should be pushing the Process Characterization program, it's their equipment and process."

"Well, in that case, why don't I just demonstrate how to do these studies and then we'll let them do it for themselves. And, at that point, once they feel more comfortable doing them, I will just witness, audit or supervise how they do it, and that will be that," Mario suggested.

"That will probably work better for them," Rob said. "They need to be shown first. This is new to them."

"What are we going to do about Harry?" Mario asked. "I know he's going to be a major roadblock in this whole effort, and just because he didn't come up with the idea. To him, this is just another impediment to producing product in a timely manner, another stumbling block from the quality assurance department. He has been undermining it by loading his engineers with work, so they don't have any time to spend on these studies. Johnny mentioned Harry changes their priorities every morning at the manufacturing engineering meeting in his office, and now its mostly just fire-fighting. Whatever problem surfaced the day before, that's what they have to work on today. They feel like they're chasing their tails."

"Well, what do you suggest we do?" asked Rob.

"I sincerely feel the only way we're going to make them do these studies correctly is by making it part of the Standard Operating Procedure for this Fuze program and making it a requirement prior to producing product for the Full Scale Production phase."

"What do you mean, Mario?"

"Rob, I think you should require them to make every piece of equipment and operation prove its capability of producing product within print specification limits prior to producing product for Full Scale Production. That way, all the equipment not capable will be categorized still under the First Article Acceptance Test phase. And, the non-capable equipment will not be accepted to produce product for Full Scale Production until it fully passes the Process Characterization qualification. We can set the requirement that each characteristic have at least a Cpk of one to be qualified for Full Scale Production."

"Hey, that sounds like it might work," Rob said enthusiastically.

"Yes," said Mario, "and Harry would not be able to override a Program Directive requiring a Cpk of one to go to Full Scale Production. He would have to commit to that! And, as a matter of fact, he probably doesn't even know what Cpk values he has at this point."

"If this is what it takes to do things right, I'll do that," Rob said. "You can count on me. You go ahead and write all the details of how the SOP should be. Also, why don't you give me a draft of a memo with the details of the Process Characterization requirements for Full Scale Production? I will then incorporate it into my Program Directive."

"I shall do that," Mario said. And as he was leaving Rob's office, Mario turned around and said, "Well, Rob, I think this is going to work well!"

His morale at this point was at an all time high. Mario had a strong hunch this plan would work. He knew if he could demonstrate how these studies were supposed to be done, all the engineers would learn, follow and hopefully run with the program. They just needed to be shown how to do it. Telling them what they should do was no way of convincing them.

And, so, the Standard Operating Procedure for Process Characterization and the Program Directive memo were written and distributed. Harry had no qualms about approving such an initiative; in reality, he had no choice because Rob, the Program Manager, had more clout than the Manufacturing Manager. So he had no recourse but to accept the SOP and allocate time for his manufacturing engineers to comply with the scheduled studies. The program of Process Characterization was passed onto the Manufacturing Department as if it were their program, but still under Mario's guidance, demonstration and coordination.

Now, with Harry's full support and his engineers' willingness to do the studies, QA and Manufacturing could finally TANGO.

———— • ————

**Change and the change process
must be coaxed, nurtured, fostered and
championed - not just announced.**

———— • ————

First Study: What is the Problem We're Fixing?

Harry got what he wanted out of the commitment to support the Process Characterization program, and that was the program itself. From now on, the program was viewed as a manufacturing engineering thing and that made him very happy.

What he didn't get, was stopping Mario from coordinating the program. The Standard Operating Procedure described in a lot of detail what needed to be done in the studies. Every study required a level of approval from Rob's organization, and that's where Mario came in - he was not going to tolerate any shortcuts. It was, after all, Mario's baby and Harry was just the stepfather.

Mario decided to first demonstrate all the necessary

steps to do the studies by actually forming a team which included the production operator, quality assurance inspector, maintenance operator, process technician and manufacturing engineer. And Mario continued with a meeting in a conference room to explain the SOP in its entirety. Then he presented the schedule so the team would be aware of the time constraints they were under. This was especially important because this was the first time they were involved on a study as a team. Immediately after that, Mario guided the team in all the details comprising a Process Characterization study.

Mario had figured that, initially, most of the work was going to be done by himself, and that was okay. The engineers needed first to see and witness how a study was done. Following that, it would be more likely they would be able to do it by themselves. He was, in fact, surprised by how fast they picked it up and how soon they started volunteering to do certain tasks.

Now Harry was very excited about initiating the program. He had distributed a memo to all his engineers and production personnel about the importance of, and the commitment necessary to pursue Process Characterization as a means to qualify for Full Scale Production.

The memo read, "... and to that avail, I have decided to establish three new positions for Process Technicians. These three individuals will assist the manufacturing engineers in the Process Characterization studies. All of you interested in the new positions, please fill an application and present it to Ned, the Production Supervisor."

Now, as Mario was walking out of his cubicle, on his way to the production floor, he had no choice but to walk in front of Harry's office.

"Mario! " he said in an unusually happy and friendly tone.

"Yes, Harry?" Mario replied and slowed his fast pace to a complete stop.

"Please, come in," he said, as he stood up and walked towards the entrance of his small office. "I've opened three positions for process technician to assist in the studies. Were you aware of that?"

He was proud again. That Texan accent was flowing strong again. And Mario could tell Harry wanted to be helpful . in the program's new deployment.

"Harry, that's a great idea. Your engineers are very busy and the process technicians will be of great assistance," Mario replied very enthusiastically. He knew that, deep, deep under that armadillo skin of Harry's, there was a soft heart that wanted to be helpful and supportive. Likewise, Harry knew they were doing the right thing to help the production process. Besides, Mario sincerely needed all the support he could get from Harry to make this program work.

"Well, I've told all my people today in the morning meeting that you're going to take them by the hand through this process. And, that all the operations are going to get fixed once and for all," Harry said, as he placed his right hand on Mario's left shoulder.

"Don't you worry about that," said Mario, "I'm going to give them my best."

"That's all we can expect from you."

Mario left Harry's office and, as he walked towards the double doors that lead to the production floor, he thought to himself, "Gee, what a change. I hope he remains like that. I can live with that."

The first team meeting was starting at ten in the morning. The first one to arrive was Angie. She was the production operator for the Lanyard Pin Press process. Angie was always in a good mood and the engineers enjoyed working with her.

"Good morning, how is my favorite troublemaker this glorious morning," she said, with a huge smile on her face.

"Good morning, Angie," Mario replied, with a smile. "I can see you had your great dose of sugar today."

"You betcha," she replied. "Somebody has to keep their shiny side up around here."

"Calm down now, Angie!"

"So, what are we doing today. What is this big meeting

all about?" Angie asked.

"We're going to start a Process Characterization study in your operation," Mario replied.

"Wow, who came up with that mouthful? I bet it was you, huh?"

"Very funny, Angie. You keep it up and I'll have you reporting to Vicky," Mario joked.

"Please, first put needles in my eyes!" replied Angie with her eyes shut, pretending she was blind as her arms went forward searching for obstacles.

She could not stand Vicky. They had been rivals in the production floor since the program started. Angie was viewed as a leader and liked by the operators. When the operators had something that bothered them, they would immediately tell Angie and she would bring it forward to the management staff in the communication meetings. Angie was a natural.

"Good morning," said Vicky, as she came into the room. "What happened Angie, you okay?" she said with a giggle.

"Oh, I was just showing Mario how they're inspecting the boards this morning." Angie's tone of voice was cocky and her smile vanished from her face.

"Be nice, be nice," Mario cautioned.

Vicky was the Quality Assurance Inspector Supervisor and she had all the inspectors reporting to her. She was excellent in establishing discipline with the inspectors. She had her area running like a German clock, in perfect unison, but she was not liked by her people. She was very well respected, but her inspectors felt she was too hard and strict. That's what kept Angie and Vicky from liking each other. While Vicky was always respectful, Angie was always making a smart remark.

Mario was just happy to have them both in the first study, because both of them were extremely open-minded and clever when it came to production. On the other hand, he knew the process technician and the two manufacturing engineers were going to be hard nuts to crack.

Freddy, the process technician, had worked with Angie before and had just been assigned to this new position. "Good morning, Freddy," Mario said as Freddy quietly came in and sat in the front row, right next to the transparency projector.

"Good morning," he replied in a soft voice.

Mario could tell he felt a little intimidated, but it was nice to see the enthusiasm he displayed in this new assignment. He had a perfectly sharpened yellow pencil, which had never been used before. And his calculator looked brand new sitting on top of its user manual; he probably had not even opened it yet. A ruler, an eraser and a sharpener were all perfectly aligned and displayed on the right hand side of his desk. Everything was meticulously aligned, an indication he was probably a perfectionist - a perfect virtue for this assignment. For an instant,

Mario was reminded of his first day in school, when he walked into class with all his newly purchased school supplies, and that unforgettable smell of new.

This assignment meant a lot to Freddy. It was a chance to move forward in his job and get away from the routine work of running production equipment. Now, he could interface with the management staff and they would have the opportunity to discover in him more useful talents. But, at that moment, it was as important that he could go in and out of the production area, and into the offices, without requesting permission from his supervisor.

At ten minutes past the hour, the two manufacturing engineers finally walked in, along with the guy from maintenance, and the meeting started.

Jay was one of the senior manufacturing engineers in the department. He had worked in other Fuze programs and that had given him plenty of experience in production, but all topics related to statistics were foreign to him. Nevertheless, he was eager to learn, for he had followed and vigorously read the reports that had come out of the overnight experiments.

On the other hand, Dave - Harry's most preferred, protected and conceited engineer - looked confused and almost lost during the presentation. He could not understand the reason for doing the studies and, as he voiced his opinions, this became apparent to all those present. "Explain to me, what is the problem we're trying to fix on this operation?" Dave demanded, almost in desperation and apparently impatient for having already gone through only half an hour of the presentation.

"Dave," Mario said, as he raised his hand to stop Dave from standing up. "Let me clarify what I said at the beginning," Mario asserted. "In a Process Characterization study, there is no particular problem we're attempting to solve. We're merely conducting an engineering study to quantify how good or how bad the equipment, operation or process is performing with respect to customer specification. Dave, it's through the study we will determine if there are problems with the operation that need fixing," Mario said.

"Yes, that's fine and dandy, Mario, but I already know where the problems are," Dave responded.

"It is not that we doubt your assessment. We want to quantify it," said Mario.

"Why don't we just focus on the equipment that's giving us trouble and fix it?" Dave insisted.

"Because we want to get undisputed proof the operation doesn't meet specifications; in other words, data."

"Okay, but why do we have to start with this one?" asked Dave.

Angie, could not stand it a second longer and she burst, "Dave, we're going to study every single one. Haven't you read Harry's memo yet?"

"Dave, put aside the problem-solving or fire-fighting approach of everyday operations," Mario said very calmly, trying to make him understand they were going to do pure engineering. They were going to measure the performance of each machine, equipment, operation and, eventually, the whole process. And if any of these didn't measure up to a Cpk of one, the new SOP standard, then it would be the focus of their optimization efforts.

"For right now, put your problem-solving skills aside and just go along for the ride," Mario repeated. "I will show you every step of the way and once we identify a problem exists, then all of us will put our problem-solving hats on and focus only on fixing the process. So just try to learn this new approach. Bare with us."

"Okay," said Dave, with a more at-ease and content tone, now that the self-imposed demand and expectation of being the problem-solver was removed.

When Mario finished his three-hour presentation, everyone appeared very enthusiastic and eager to proceed. He realized then the team was in tune. So they took a break as a group to eat lunch in the cafeteria and, afterwards, they proceeded to the production floor to start the first study.

———————— • ————————

Before looking for a solution, it is best to first systematically find common ground for understanding what the problem truly is and what caused it.

———————— • ————————

A 99.73 Percent First-Pass Yield

The first thing the manufacturing engineers wanted to do was to start making modifications to the equipment setup and run experiments. The first thing they, as a team, had to do, according to the SOP, was identify all variables in the process through a brainstorming session. The manufacturing engineers needed, first, to have a good understanding of the process and how it worked, before they could be useful in fixing it. But equally important, they needed to determine how capable it was in its ability to produce product within customer specification limits. And that required that they quantify its Cpk index.

The Cpk is an index of process capability, and it quantifies the ability of the process to produce product within specification limits. The larger the Cpk value, the better the process; that is, the more uniform and repeatable the process. The smaller the Cpk value, the worse the process and the more variability it will have in producing within specification limits.

Initially, the SOP required a Cpk of one to go into Full Scale Production. This implied a first pass yield of at least 99.73 percent; that is, 99.73 percent of product must be within customer specification to start Full Scale Production. If after conducting the Process Characterization study this level was not achieved, then the operation would remain in First Article Acceptance Test (FAAT) phase and could not produce product for the Full Scale Production. This implied they could not ship product to the customer.

Harry didn't know he had committed his Fuze process to deliver at Full Scale Production levels. Mario didn't think even Rob realized what he had committed to, either - but both had already signed the document. And the document had already been presented to the customer for approval. Of course, the customer had agreed immediately; not particularly surprising, given the commitment had come from the vendor (the Fuze program) without the customer's initial request. Now there was no stepping back from the commitment. They had to have those yields before producing. Now the only choice was to give it their undivided focus and full support. And that was exactly what they needed to make it work.

The first study had started remarkably well and the team was working harmoniously under the full support of management. The operation and equipment in the first study selected was not the simplest, but it was certainly not the most difficult either. It was one Mario suspected would guarantee success for this first team. That was the simple reason for its selection. They needed to start with a success story and an example everyone could look up to and follow in future studies. At the same time, once they completed and documented one study, there would be no one who could deny the applicability or the results of the process characterization approach in the Fuze program.

As the team met in the production area, Mario proceeded to inform them that, initially, he was going to demonstrate every step and he just wanted them to pay close attention to what he was doing, and to ask any questions they had.

Dave said, "I thought WE were the ones doing the study?"

"Yes, YOU will do the study, but first I will do everything for one single characteristic, so you guys can learn the approach."

"Okay, that's better," Dave said.

Mario continued, "I will show you every step with the first characteristic. This operation has about six of them. You guys will do the rest," Mario said. "But remember, you guys need to ask questions, so you can learn."

"Okay, not a problem," said Dave, as everybody else nodded their heads in approval.

And so, Mario started the whole procedure. First, the team rank-ordered all the independent variables according to their influence. Then, they conducted a Repeatability and Reproducibility study with the gauge they were going to use to measure the first characteristic. And to give them a feel of what doing the study was like, Mario got them involved in taking the measurements and playing the role of the operators. Getting them involved finally triggered a few questions.

"Why are we taking repeated measurements?" Freddy asked.

"That's the only way we can quantify the variability produced by the operator," said Mario patiently.

"But why do we have to use ten parts, can't we use just five?" said Angie. She was interested in speeding things up.

"Usually, the more data the better, but we could still have used five. It's just that all the formulas will change because the constants used are for ten parts," replied Mario.

"I think five parts are too few, not too representative of our process volume," said Vicky. "We will be inspecting about 550 units everyday in the near future."

The momentum of the team was building up as they got involved in more details of the study. Mario knew the questions would become more challenging later.

"I don't understand why you're using the product tolerance instead of the gauge tolerance," Dave complained. "I thought we were trying to study the gauge, not the product at this point?"

"You're absolutely right," Mario said, "we're studying the gauge, not the product, but if we compare the gauge against its own tolerance, it's probably okay. But that's not our concern. What we want to know is whether we have selected the right gauge to measure our product. So we need to know what percentage of the tolerance of the product is consumed by the variability in the gauge. That will tell us whether the gauge is good or not, for the measurements we want to make."

The team moved forward quickly and, as they quantified the characteristic, they found it extremely capable for their requirements. Its Cpk value was 2.83 and the data demonstrated it was well under statistical control. With nothing else to do about that particular characteristic, the team proceeded with the next characteristics following the same approach Mario had just shown them.

They were not so lucky. The second characteristic failed miserably. It did not appear to be stable and its Cpk value was 0.82; definitely below their minimum of one.

At this point, they decided to stop for the day and start fresh the following morning. It had been a long busy day for all of them. "We'll meet in the conference room tomorrow at eight and start fresh with a brainstorming session," Mario told them.

"It sounds like a plan," said Vicky, and everybody agreed.

They had accomplished a lot for the first day. But one thing Mario was particularly excited about was he no longer needed to run overnight experiments under strict secrecy and silence, as he had had to do before. Now, he could request equipment time during first shift, do the experiments in broad daylight and nobody had to work overtime. That idea felt good.

The following morning the team reconvened in the conference room and started with a brainstorming session. The purpose was to theorize and generate ideas about why the equipment had given them lousy results. They came up with a few good theories and they decided to try them in an experiment. After spending most of the morning changing settings and running units they were unable to make any significant improvements.

"Gee, what are we doing wrong?" asked Vicky.

"I have no idea," said Dave, with a puzzled look on his face. "I thought these variables would have a strong impact on the results."

"Let's go back to the drawing board," Mario said.

And, almost concurrently, Angie remarked, "About the only thing we haven't tried is measuring every piece part in the assembly." Her tone had been a touch sarcastic and everybody looked at her weird. Heads had not moved, only their eyes pointed at Angie. And, in everybody's face, there was this puzzled look which seemed to be morphing into a grin, as if they had missed the most obvious of things.

Vicky broke the silence. "That can't be," she said. But her remark was expected, she did not like Angie.

"Well, she may not be too far off," said Jay.

"I agree, we haven't tried that yet," said Dave, in defense of Angie.

"Good!" said Freddy, giving a thumbs up to Angie.

"Let's try it," Mario said, as they all stopped whatever they were doing and started to get to it.

The team had split the piece parts amongst themselves and everyone had a different piece part to measure. To their shock, they discovered that one piece part was completely out of tolerance.

"How could that be?" they asked themselves. All the piece-parts were coming from their parts warehouse and they knew they had already been sample-inspected by Incoming Quality Assurance.

It had been Vicky's piece parts which had measured out of tolerance. And not just a few of them, but 100 percent of them out of tolerance! In short, they had been given the wrong piece parts to assemble.

"Don't tell me that Incoming is also totally screwed up!" Jay remarked, totally disappointed.

This surprise completely united the team. It was almost like an instant bonding. Now they were completely unified, as if all of them were facing a common enemy. Now it was them, the Fuze team, against the Incoming Quality Assurance Department.

Since this was a quality issue, Mario decided to take the initiative and immediately placed a call to Dean, the Incoming QA representative for their parts.

Dean had been on the job for over a year now. Previously, he had been with Ford, as a Supplier Quality Assurance Manager, but he had grown tired of traveling and he had decided to take a cut in pay and take the position of Supervisor of Incoming Quality Assurance with the company. He had also been fed up with the cold weather in Detroit and, in contrast, sunny Arizona had been very appealing to him. Dean was a practical joker and was always telling jokes, and always in a good mood.

On one occasion, some six months before, Dean had gotten a lot of heat for a practical joke about his pay, and it had almost gotten another person fired. Dean had been absent on a Friday, the day they used to get paid, and his paycheck had been saved by the secretary of his department. The following Tuesday, when he came back to work, the secretary had given him his check. As Dean was walking down the hall, a very unhappy employee had walked by him at the same moment that Dean had opened the envelope. Upon removing the check from the envelope, Dean had exclaimed, "Wow!" And he had stared at the check as he held it with both hands. It was then the unhappy employee, curious about Dean's surprise, had asked him, "What's that?" And Dean, without slowing his pace, had told the guy, "This is a bonus check! Haven't you gotten one?"

Of course, the employee - who had been very unhappy and who had been asking to get a raise for a long time and had been denied one - went ballistic, and walked off quickly to his desk to look for his bonus check. Not finding one, he went to ask the secretary and had finally realized he had not gotten one. He was fuming! The employee went directly into the SQA manager's office and without knocking, burst in and started screaming and cussing, demanding to know why he had not gotten a bonus check! The boss, not knowing where this maniac was coming from - with this crazy idea that he was supposed to get a bonus check, when they had not given bonuses to anybody - attempted to calm him down. The enraged employee would not stop yelling.

Once he managed to calm the guy down, the boss asked him where he had gotten the idea that bonuses were being given, and the poor guy explained the incident in the hall with Dean. Needless to say, both Dean and the guy had almost gotten fired for that incident. The story had traveled like wildfire through the grapevine and, rightfully or wrongfully so, had established Dean's reputation as a practical joker.

Dean was at his desk when the phone rang. His first reaction was that Mario was totally crazy. Despite his well-earned reputation, Dean was extremely proud of his work and his integrity was definitely nothing to joke about. Mario told him to come immediately to the Fuze area because, if it was the vendor's fault, they needed this vendor to contain the problem as soon as possible, explain what had happened and start sending good parts again. The team had already spent the whole morning and the previous afternoon studying a process whose piece parts were defective. They couldn't afford to lose more precious time!

Fortunately, Dean came rather quickly. He was prompt, especially when his ass was on the line. He came prepared with piece-part prints and the sample inspection reports done by his inspectors. "Hi, where are the parts?" he asked.

"Follow me, they're on the production floor," Mario said.

After measuring a few parts, Dean could not believe all of them were the wrong dimension. "But this incoming inspection report shows all the samples passed inspection," he said. "This doesn't make any sense."

"Well, Dean, if we're going to have to measure every piece part you send us, we're screwed," said Mario.

"Don't jump to conclusions, Mario, let me check what happened here."

"What can I say? We've just spent two days working on this operation, just to find out the parts are bad!" exclaimed Mario.

"Don't worry. You'll have good parts by tomorrow. Even if I have to fly there to get them," Dean said, as he was starting to leave the area.

"You'll call me back?"

"In one hour," Dean assured Mario.

It was amazing! If they had not started the Process Characterization study, probably nobody would have detected a piece part was out of tolerance, and they could have potentially built thousands of units before realizing they were defective.

The team was feeling just great! They had solved a potential problem in the program. The following day Dean came back with good parts. The piece parts given to them before had been the wrong part number altogether; apparently, just an internal mistake from either the Materiel department or the warehouse personnel. The piece parts inspected by Incoming were correct and the vendor did not have a problem.

On the third day, the team continued their study and the Cpk for that response improved to acceptable levels. They proceeded that day studying the next three characteristics and their Cpk's exceeded the goals. Now all they had to do was just study the final characteristic and the whole Lanyard Assembly Operation would be completely characterized with a yield of about 99.73 percent.

The last characteristic didn't appear to be as easy as the previous ones. It was going to require some experiments to really optimize this characteristic.

The Wire Cut & Bond equipment was supposed to unwind stainless steel rope wire from a stock coil to a particular length. Then it cut and bonded the ends of the wire, so the twisted wire strands would not come undone. Every single strand had to be bonded, forming a nice round smooth ball. They figured a few experiments would have to be tried to find the optimum settings for the Wire Cut & Bond equipment and still preserve the length required.

Upon determining its capability, the team realized the initial equipment setup and variables were not guaranteeing the yield they were committed to achieving. Its current long term yield was estimated to be in the neighborhood of about 82 percent.

After running a couple of experiments, a significant improvement was achieved by the team and the yield was increased to about 94 percent. They still had about 6 percent of the units with problems, with strands unwinding and bonds not forming a uniform surface. These experiments took a long time because their nature was time consuming and because the team lacked a thorough understanding of the process. This was expected. The team was going through the learning curve. In the past, this learning curve had usually been spread out over the production life of a product; that is, correct and learn the process as product was being produced. What the Process Characterization program was attempting to do was force the team through the learning curve now, before they started producing product on a large scale.

The team was on the fourth day of studying the Lanyard Assembly process when, all of a sudden, Harry made an entrance in the production area while the team was busy changing some of the equipment parameters, getting ready for another treatment.

"Goddammit! I've seen you guys playing with that piece of equipment for the last three days now, and you still can't get it to work," he hollered.

Mario didn't know where Harry was coming from, being all upset like that. But being the senior in the group and the one not reporting to Harry, Mario came to the defense of the team. "We've made great improvements in the last three days and we're almost finished. The yield on this final characteristic has already been improved to 94 percent," Mario said quickly.

"We have not produced any assemblies for the past three days and I have the operators there, doing nothing!" Harry replied, still huffing and puffing. "We will have to ramp up to 550 units per day and you guys are still messing with the same equipment."

"Well, Harry, we have already increased the yield to 94 percent from about 82 percent, and have already characterized all other characteristics. All we need is just one more response and the whole assembly will have a perfect yield of 99 percent," said Mario.

"This equipment is not a priority. I can live with the 94 percent," Harry continued. "I want you, Dave and Jay, to stop what you're doing and come with me. The encapsulation process is totally screwed-up, and I want both of you to work on that one. Now!"

The two engineers had no choice but to stop and start walking towards the encapsulation area.

So Mario asked Harry, "What happened at encapsulation that makes it a priority now?"

"Yesterday the defect rate increased from 12 to 35 units. QA is rejecting almost three times as much as before. This is definitely a major problem!" Harry replied.

"Well, Harry, we're very close to finishing here, and I don't see why we should stop now!"

"This piece of equipment is already at 94 percent," Harry remarked. "I don't know how much you want to improve it! I need my people to work on the real problems, and encapsulation has a higher priority right now."

It was typical of Harry to make his engineers drop everything they were doing to spend their time fire-fighting. Somehow, he felt his engineers had to work on whatever the issue of the day was; whether they were chasing their tail or not.

"Harry, we have committed to increase the Cpk of every operation to a value of one and, concurrently, the first pass yield has to agree with a 99.73 percent before we can produce for FSP."

"I'm aware of that," Harry said.

"If we're stopping this study at this point we will have one defective lanyard for every twenty we do. At that rate, we will need to devote more engineering time to dispose of defective units and hire extra manpower for rework and inspection. If you think you're short on engineers now, with unfinished processes like this one, they won't have time to do any engineering; they will be fire-fighting forever," Mario said without flinching.

"Well, goddammit, every time that I tell you what I want my engineers to do, you goddam contradict me!" Harry turned abruptly and started back to his office.

At that instant, Mario thought, "There's no way anything is going to be accomplished with this guy in charge of engineering!" But Mario also had a hunch the facts Harry was throwing at his face were once again wrong. With his disregard for data, Harry was pretty good at reaching the wrong conclusion most of the time.

So Mario decided to follow Dave and Jay who, by now, were probably already well on their way to starting their new assignment. He went into the encapsulation area and talked to the operator. Mario asked the operator to let him look at his records for the week's daily outputs. Then Mario talked to the inspector of the operation which immediately followed encapsulation and asked for information about the reject categories, defects and data for the week's worth of inspection.

With all the facts in his possession, and after reviewing the data, Mario's suspicions were confirmed and this made him even more furious! As he walked back to his cubicle, Mario was thinking, "This darn Texan can sure add, but he can't divide worth a shit!"

Looking at three weeks'-worth of data, Mario saw the production rates fluctuated from 98 to 580 units per day. The number of units rejected by the inspector fluctuated from 10 all the way to 40 per day. Calculating the loss in yield for the area, the average was about 5 ± 2 percent; therefore, the yield loss had to be between 3 and 7 percent. Looking at the previous day's production rate, only 315 units were sent for inspection, of which 12 units were rejected for encapsulation problems. That was about a 4 percent yield loss. The day before, they produced about 535 units and inspection rejected 35; that was about a 6.5 percent yield loss.

In essence, Mario discovered the increase in rejects from 12 to 35, that Harry claimed was a major problem, was just random variation in the process. In other words, there was no significant difference between the performance of the encapsulation process from one day to the next. And there was no higher rate of rejection of units by inspection. But Harry was forcing his engineers to drop everything they were doing to react to simple random variation, making them believe it was a catastrophic problem!

"The sad thing," Mario thought, "is the yield of the encapsulation process is almost identical to the Lanyard Assembly operation, and the team has been forced to stop its study, to work on something that is definitely not a priority."

This was classic fire-fighting at its best.

Angry and frustrated, Mario decided to put all his findings on a transparency foil and immediately called the program management to a meeting. He didn't want anything to stop the momentum of the Process Characterization studies and, most definitely, nothing as senseless as making the engineers react to random variation.

The urgency of the meeting notice generated great participation. When Mario presented the facts, the shit hit the fan. Harry was extremely embarrassed and humiliated, and ready to chew out Ned, his Production Supervisor. It was Ned who presented him with the problem in the morning communication meeting. It was a typical case of reacting to unfounded opinions, with no data to back it up.

Needless to say, the team resumed its focus on the Lanyard Assembly operation and Harry did not intervene for the next few months in the schedule of studies. The Lanyard Assembly operation's capability and its yields were increased to exceed the FSP goals.

In the following months, thanks to the Process Characterization program, great advances in yields were made on the Fuze program.

———————— • ————————

Data, data, data.
All decisions have to be backed up with data and statistically significant differences.

———————— • ————————

Welcome the Ayatollah of Process Controla

Over thirty-five studies were done in a period of a few months. Modifications to equipment, fixtures, tools and gauges were extensively carried-out by the teams as they found their influence on the overall capability of a process.

Statistically-designed experiments were conducted on numerous operations and the manufacturing engineers were involved completely throughout the whole process.

Some machines and processes got optimized to very high levels, far exceeding the Cpk goal of one. The manufacturing engineers found themselves doing less and less fire-fighting; and, more and more, they were involved in Process Characterization studies.

But Harry still had a stone in his shoe.

Although the Process Characterization program was now their program, it was still mainly directed and controlled by Mario. In many instances, when the study required improvement, Harry was still reluctant to increase the first pass yield to 99.73 percent and very content with a yield above 90 percent. Harry still carried a strong grudge from the incident in the encapsulation area, when he had made his engineers drop everything they were doing to react to random variation. He would have preferred Mario had not presented his findings in front of the whole program management.

After a few minor encounters, Harry decided to look for somebody with strong qualifications he could hire to report directly to him. He wanted someone to challenge Mario's program domination and his technical knowledge of statistical methods. At the same time, having a new individual reporting directly to him would give Harry the chance to fully influence the course of action in the studies. Harry could then have the studies end at his convenience; not at all like what was currently occurring, which was to let the data do the talking and have the studies end when the goals were achieved.

One day, out of the blue, Harry came to Mario's cubicle and cheerfully said, "How are you today?"

Mario answered, "Fine, Harry, and you?"

"Great! Just today I finally found a person that I'm going to bring into the program. I spoke with his father. His father is a famous consultant, a guru in SPC; he tells me that his son has a Master's degree in statistics and he knows as much as he does, and that he's looking for a job."

"Well that's great, Harry!"

"Now, I've found someone that's going to challenge you, Mario."

Mario didn't know what to make of what Harry said: should he be happy, should he be sad, should he be afraid? Mario still thought, however, that Harry's real or primary motive was to have somebody challenge all of his decisions and course of action in the studies.

A couple of seconds lapsed and Mario was still staring at Harry. "Now I want to see what you're going to do," Harry said as he turned around and left Mario's cubicle.

It was a spooky feeling for Mario, "Am I such a threat to Harry? I'm doing the best I can to help the program. I'm giving all my best to the program and I'm putting in an extra effort to make it as perfect as possible, so we can all profit from the rewards. I could care less who does the studies, as long as they're done correctly and as long as we're not cheating ourselves, either by mistake or by ignorance on the subject of applied statistics. I don't expect rewards for myself from these studies; I just want the yields to be as high as possible, so we can all hold on to our jobs."

Harry didn't seem to see it the same way. To Harry it was still Mario against him, QA against Manufacturing. Or, as

Harry eloquently called it: a pissing contest.

Unfortunately for Harry, he didn't have an open requisition to hire an extra engineer on his staff. So he convinced the Central Engineering Manager, John Eikes, to hire this new engineer and put him on loan to the Fuze program, reporting directly to both John and himself.

The Central Engineering department was comprised of a pool of design, manufacturing, process and product engineers who were involved in a variety of programs. Occasionally, some of those engineers would go on temporary assignment, for one or two years, where they could be involved in a program that reported concurrently to Central Engineering. Once the program advanced into the production phases, those engineers would go back to Central Engineering ready for another assignment.

The story of Harry hiring somebody to challenge Mario metamorphosed through the grapevine into Harry hiring somebody to eliminate Mario and his function from the program. The rumor went around that Harry was hiring a guru in statistics and manufacturing, and that brought a lot of visitors with questions to Mario's cubicle. Mario reassured them it was Harry's last-straw attempt at controlling the Fuze process.

A month later the new engineer was hired and, after his initial orientation, John, the Central Engineering Manager, had the courtesy of bringing him down to the offices and introducing him to everybody. They went from cubicle to cubicle doing the introductions. When they arrived at Mario's cubicle, John said, "Good afternoon, Mario, I would like to introduce Eddy Batra, he is going to join the program and be your counterpart in the Manufacturing department; he'll be reporting to Harry."

"Very nice to meet you," Mario said.

"Nice to meet you, too," Eddy responded as he extended his right hand.

Mario shook hands with him and John continued, "Eddy is the son of the famous SPC guru Kenny Batra. You have probably read some of his books."

"Of course," Mario said.

"I would like you to train Eddy in the whole SPC program you've put together here, until he gets familiar with the Fuze program."

"I'll be glad to do that," affirmed Mario.

"He doesn't have any experience with production or manufacturing; he comes from the business side." And then, turning to Eddy, John said, "Mario is our expert in statistical methods, so I leave you in good hands."

Mario's curiosity was immediately triggered by John's comments, so he asked Eddy, "What is your background in statistics?"

"Not much experience, but I'm looking forward to

learning a lot from you," Eddy finished his sentence and stared at Mario quietly.

Realizing that was it, that there would be no more comments, Mario said, "Welcome to the program." And he gave Eddy a polite smile.

Eddy smiled back and said, "Thank you, it was very nice meeting you, too."

Eddy's response left a serious doubt in Mario's mind about his experience with applied statistics, "Maybe he really is very well versed on the subject, but he doesn't want to admit it, so as to test my ability. Or maybe he truly means he has no experience; or maybe he means he has no experience because he has just finished his Master's degree. Or is it really true he doesn't have any background in statistics?" The whole thing was very puzzling to Mario.

The following day Eddy arrived at Mario's cubicle at 8:00 AM sharp, with two cups of coffee in his hands. He was very well dressed, with a full pin stripe suit, crisp and heavily-starched; 100 percent Pima cotton white shirt and a Brooks Brothers' silk tie. The knot on his tie was perfectly constructed - not to the right, not to the left, as is usually the case, but exactly centered and tight.

"Good morning, I thought you might want to start the day with some coffee," Eddy said.

His pronunciation of the English language was excellent. Mario could not detect any trace of a foreign accent. He had made a conscious effort to detect one because anybody who saw Eddy would probably assume he was from India. It turned out his parents had arrived from India, but he had been born and bred in Chicago.

"Thank you, I definitely need that," Mario responded.

They spent most of the day together and Mario gave Eddy a thorough orientation of the production area, and the assembly and test of Fuzes. To his astonishment, Mario found that Eddy only had a Bachelor of Arts in Business Administration; he didn't have a Masters' degree in anything and he definitely had not mastered statistics!

Nevertheless, what Mario saw was an individual with a vigorous desire to learn what his father did truly master. And his ability to remember technical terms was incredible! After spending the whole day explaining the process, the machines and the statistical methods they were using, Mario was amazed at how much Eddy had retained.

By the end of the day, Mario realized he had gained a friend, instead of the antagonistic colleague Harry had intended. Mario found an individual who truly had a great potential for becoming an asset to the program. If Eddy could learn to apply statistics as well as he could retain technical concepts, he would be in great shape.

Eddy lacked formal training in statistics, but that was going to be Mario's personal challenge. That is, Mario was going to share his knowledge with Eddy so the manufacturing department would have somebody who could eventually lead and coordinate the Process Characterization program.

In the following eight weeks Mario took Eddy through almost all stages of the Process Characterization methodology and lectured him on specific statistical methods. Eddy also underwent formal training with the PhD Consultant from the Communication Division. Eddy had had no choice on that. John had scheduled him to attend those seminars.

Eddy had also been involved in implementing certain control charts, collecting data, and analyzing multiple studies. But, it was obvious, he was not fully prepared to lead a study from the beginning, or even a problem-solving effort, without some guidance or coaching. Nevertheless, his eagerness to just jump out of the nest and fly solo was overwhelming. He had built up his confidence and, contrary to Mario's advice, he took an assignment with Harry.

Mario knew Eddy had strong potential, but although he had learned everything Mario had taught him, he had not learned everything Mario knew. He still needed experience and maturity on the subject; something only time, exposure and fail- ure teaches. And Eddy didn't realize his exposure to the appli- cation of statistical methods had been sheltered and protected by Mario's presence in all past events. Now, on his first solo flight, there would be no safety net. Mario knew there was no way Harry would allow him to intervene in Eddy's new assign- ment.

Even though Eddy was surrounded by technical people who were supposed to understand the subject, Eddy's thorough exposure these past few weeks had given him a cockiness that came from realizing not everybody understood or was comfortable with statistics. Thirsty for his first solo assignment, Eddy jumped at the opportunity and, now, on top of it all, Harry had pressured him to start the assignment prematurely.

Harry was still in need of somebody who could calm his thirst for solving the recurrent problems that were intermittently surfacing in operations and processes that still had not undergone the Process Characterization studies. Although these studies were on the schedule, Harry was always pushing his engineers to skip steps and dictating they take shortcuts and go straight to making changes in the process, prior to truly and sincerely understanding the process. Now, Harry had his own SPC coordinator to lead the way, so he assigned Eddy to his own project of reducing the high incidence of defects that were surfacing at the wave soldering area.

What had jump-started an increase in wave solder defects was that a printed circuit board supplier, PC Teck - which used to sell them boards, but had been removed from the suppliers' list because of poor quality, even though PC Teck's boards were half the other suppliers' price - had found a way of coming back to the program, once again as a supplier of boards. PC Teck had complained that removing them as a preferred vendor would potentially be detrimental to their business. But vast amounts of past evidence, in the form of control charts and comparative analysis, had proven this supplier's boards were significantly inferior in quality when compared to other suppliers. And now, PC Teck had given Harry a large lot of boards for evaluation and Harry had just injected them once again into the production line.

For months, the program had been using GrafCo Research boards exclusively, and the wave solder machine had already been optimized and was running virtually defect-free. In an attempt to lower costs, Harry decided to use Eddy to lead a project for reducing solder defects in the wave solder process.

To that effect, Harry wrote a memo that said: "...and the number of defects in the wave solder area has increased to an average of 36 per board. A team led by Eddy Batra (our new SPC Coordinator), Chris Leffew, and Robert Mack will tackle the problem."

The number of defects had sky-rocketed, but it was due to the PC Teck boards and Eddy did not know that; nor had he been made aware of the previous problems associated with the boards. So, along with a manufacturing engineer and a process technician, Eddy embarked on trying to improve the process.

They made but a few mistakes in their approach to the whole assignment, but these were truly detrimental mistakes. First, a Variable Search approach was taken which, by its very nature, would not detect interaction between variables in the process - and there had been some levels of interaction detected before. Then, sample sizes were set too low, when it was essential to obtain precision in the results of attribute data. But by far, the most detrimental blunder was not testing if the behavior of the PC Teck boards was under statistical control.

They missed that all together! The fact was those boards were totally unstable. They had erratic defect levels that changed from board to board, and even on consecutive boards. The board-to-board variability was so large it would mask every effect in the experiments. And in all cases, the experiments were inconclusive; indicating the error was too large and giving the perception that none of the process variables, which had been the subject of experimentation, were influential.

For two weeks, experiment after experiment was done, but nothing was accomplished. The operators and inspectors were tired of changing setups in the wave solder equipment and tired of inspecting boards; all to find nothing! So they jokingly branded Eddy the "Ayatollah of Process Controla."

Harry was equally frustrated because his SPC Coordinator had been unable to fix his problem and now was being branded with a nickname. So, Harry decided to transfer Eddy back to the Central Engineering Department. There Eddy lasted about six months in the program and was later reassigned to implement Control Charts in another program. But, despite it all, Mario and Eddy became very good friends.

On the other hand, the PC Teck supplier was eliminated altogether from supplying boards to the company, thus losing its major account. And two months later, Mario heard the PC Teck plant had mysteriously caught fire and burned to a crisp.

_____ • _____

Technical knowledge alone is not sufficient. Knowledge

**compounded by experience,
and adherence to a time-tested and proven methodology,
together are the keys to effective process characterization
and optimization.**

_____ • _____

Fourteen in Five

At the end of the First Article Acceptance Test (FAAT) or pre-production phase, 150 units were delivered to the customer for full testing. At the same time, the teams were finalizing the Process Characterization studies and the Cpk's were all higher than one. Some equipment was overwhelmingly capable and the complete Fuze manufacturing process had a process capability index higher than one. The Fuze program was ready for the Full Scale Production phase and they were just waiting for the FAAT results to pass all the testing done by the customer.

It was a Friday, in the middle of a hot Arizona summer, when the temperature reaches over 116 degrees Fahrenheit in the shade - when steering wheels are barely touchable and wearing dark glasses is a full-time necessity, just to avoid the blinding glare of the sun. Mario arrived at work to find out the Fuze program had been shut down by the customer. They had failed the FAAT! Apparently, some units had failed at cold temperature.

All the work they had done for months came to a screeching halt.

As Mario walked through the long corridor that would take him to the production area on one side, and to the staff offices on the other, many of the operators were on their way home. Their heads were down and they were visibly confused with the explanation they had been given. The bottom line for them was they had to go home for an undetermined time, with minimum pay, facing the hardship of making ends meet.

Some operators were bitter. In their minds, the engineers were the bright people who had gone to college to get a degree and some had even gone further for higher degrees. But all these engineers could do was be picky, telling them how to do their work, how to build it and how to inspect it. Then they would explain why this and why that; they always had a reason and, of course, they would use technical language - engineering lingo - to answer their questions. But, in the end, when the units failed, it was them, the operators who had to go home and wait. The engineers would continue working and would still have a job and get paid, regardless of who was really responsible for the shut-down. Of course this was not altogether true, but that's what the operators believed, and that's exactly how they felt that dreadful morning.

As Mario walked into the staff offices, all the engineers were standing, their heads sticking out of their cubicles, as if they were waiting for somebody. Their faces revealed their weariness and they had all stopped working as if it was all over.

Mario walked past his cubicle on his way directly to Rob's office. "Hi Rob, what's going on?"

"Six units failed to open at cold and ambient temperatures. Their forces exceeded the 100 pound-force limit, and we've been shut down," Rob replied.

"So what now?" asked Mario

"Two things. First, we need to explain to the customer what went wrong and then, we need to find a solution so it won't happen again. Once that's all done, then we can initiate a retest plan," Rob said.

At that point, Mario knew the different departments most likely were going to initiate actions, tests and experiments to correct the problem. He also knew being in the role of statistical methods liaison with the customer, he would have to explain each and every experiment to their statisticians, should they decide to bring them in. Mario also assumed each department - Design, Manufacturing, Engineering, Production and Quality - might try to prove or justify they were not responsible for the failure. And in the act of covering their ass, they might run experiments with conflicting results. So, foreseeing he may have to explain the results of conflicting experiments, Mario decided to offer his services to coordinate all the experiments that would be conducted to correct the problem and, in this way, have control over the statistical validation of the experiments.

Immediately after leaving Rob's office, Mario sent a memo inviting all the staff of the different departments and asked the secretary to telephone everybody on the distribution list, to ensure they would come to the meeting.

The meeting was scheduled for one o'clock and most of those invited came early. Representing the Manufacturing department were Dave and Fred, both Engineers. Production was represented by Ned, the Production Supervisor; he had invited two operators. Test Engineering had sent a Senior Test Engineer responsible for the Functional Tester. Central Engineering had sent six people in total and two of them were from design: a younger engineer named Dale, and Bob, the one responsible for the design of the fuze itself. Dale was just out of college and this was his first assignment. Representing Quality Assurance were Mark, the Production Quality Supervisor; Vicky, the QA Inspector Supervisor; and Phil, a Quality Engineer.

With most of his peers present, Mario opened the meeting, "You must know by now we have failed the FAAT, and for the next few weeks a lot of us are going to be conducting experiments to find the reason we failed the FAAT, and we're going to be looking for a solution to the problem. Some of the experiments are going to have results that are going to be very conflicting with results others have gotten. I'm going to be in charge of coordinating and analyzing all the experiments so we show our customer a consistent approach. If you're planning an experiment, I'm going to ask you to let me know before you run it so I can assist you in designing it and make it statistically sound."

"Why you?" somebody yelled from the back.

Mario didn't even notice who asked the question, but he responded, "This is the time when we have to demonstrate to our customer we can do things consistently, as a team. We just showed them we cannot produce it consistently."

Then he proceeded to ask them if anybody had an objection with him coordinating all the experiments. Luckily, nobody else had an objection. By virtue of that, Mario proceeded to tell them, "Since we have most of the departments and the know-how for building the fuze represented here, let's start a brainstorming session so we can initiate our first experiment."

Mario was amazed at how receptive they were. Some even expressed their satisfaction that somebody had decided to take charge of the matter.

"I wish somebody had taken charge when we had corrosion crystals growing in the missile program. We were just going at it from every angle with no direction," said Dave.

After a few minutes, Mario recaptured their attention by explaining the rules they were to follow for doing a brainstorming session. "How many of you have been involved in a brainstorming session before?" Mario inquired. To his surprise, only two people acknowledged their previous experience with brainstorming.

Mario helped the group move forward by presenting and discussing problems versus symptoms. He was able to reach a consensus for the brainstorming topic and continued to fill-in the Cause and Effect diagram he had drawn on the blackboard. The brainstorming had started very well and was moving in an organized manner until the first individual mentioned the o-ring internal diameter was the wrong size. At that point, people started arguing and pandemonium ensued.

"What do you mean the o-ring is the wrong size?" asked Bob.

"When the operators try to close the units, the o-ring is coming out of the groove," replied Dave.

"Well, that's because the operators are not trained well," said Bob.

"No operator does an operation in this program if they have not been certified for workmanship," exclaimed Ned, furious with the accusation of the design people.

"The reason the units don't open at a high force has to be related to the o-ring, but it could be the wrong material, too," said Mark.

"No, we're using the right material. Viton is the same material we used on the previous Fuze," Bob responded. "The problem is more related to the force the operators place when closing the units. This is done manually."

"Don't you guys go through a design review before they finalize the materials list?" asked Ned.

"I think the lubricant is hardening at a cold temperature and that locks the unit from opening at a lower force," added Jay.

"Well, if that's the case," responded Vicky, "then, maybe, we should try different lubricants, to see which one works."

"I think the lubricant and the o-ring, when they're closed by the operators, rotate and twist and increase in diameter, and that locks the units, requiring more force to open them," suggested Freddy.

"We can fix that by curing the units," replied Phil. "Apply temperature and it will go back to its original position."

"Yeah, but that's a non-value-added operation," said Mark. "You don't even know what caused the problem and you're already adding a patch to it."

"Do the assembly instructions explain the technique on how to hold the o-rings when they close the units?" asked Bob. "Or does each operator do what they want?"

"Are you talking to me?" said Mark, looking straight at

Bob and doing his best to imitate Robert de Niro.

"Well, don't the operators report to you?" asked Bob.

"Yes, but I don't write the assembly instructions," replied Mark.

"Who writes the assembly instructions?" asked Bob again.

After a few more minutes spent on nothing but finger-pointing and mutual accusations, Mario called the whole group to order and presented an alternative, "All of you probably have in your own minds an idea of what caused the failure and what the solution for the units to open at a lower force is. Some of you may be absolutely correct, but some of your ideas may be totally wrong. We're not here to argue, because that could take until hell freezes over. We're here to share our ideas, not to fight about them."

Then Mario showed them a list of everybody's name and asked them, one by one, to present their theory or idea. And he insisted that during their time, nobody would interrupt until all had spoken and all ideas had been exhausted.

"What I'm going to do is design an experiment in which we will try all ideas, all of them. And we will let the data do the talking. Let the data show us what ideas are right or wrong," Mario affirmed. And he looked around to see if anybody was in disagreement.

"Well, no," said Bob, "but are you going to try everybody's idea?"

"Leave that to me, Bob."

So Mario proceeded name by name and idea after idea. And they were more receptive to this approach and also more respectful of everybody's time to talk.

Once he disclosed, merged and polished all ideas, Mario showed them how to define the variables and their respective levels to produce the treatments they were to include in the experiment. From the whole group, only two people had previously been involved in running factorial designs. For everyone else, this was the first time they had been exposed to this approach.

Bob, the senior design engineer, had been designing fuzes for nearly two decades and he was convinced, and insisted, the reason for the high opening force was due to the operators. "They are closing the units in such a way that it locks the units," he said.

"Bob," Mario said, "you're an experienced designer, right?"

"Yes," Bob replied.

"Well, why don't you design another way of assembling the covers with the o-ring and lubricant, eliminating the operator's influence you claim."

"Well, I can certainly do that," he took Mario's challenge with pride.

"We will call this variable the Operator's Technique and we can test your theory," Mario said.

"Okay, its a deal," Bob agreed.

"We will run some units with the current way the operators use and then with your method of assembly, and we'll call it Bob's Method," Mario was serious.

"You got it," replied Bob.

They came up with six variables at two levels each. Upon drawing the design matrix for the experiment, Mario noticed that most people were lost; but he had no choice. He had to continue because, at this point, there was no time to teach them. Then, when they were defining all the treatments, they found a constraint. They would be unable to obtain o-rings of the same material in different diameters in the short time they had. Getting different diameters would require vendor involvement. So, instead, Mario decided to first combine the o-ring material and the o-ring diameter into the o-ring type, which would allow for combinations of different materials and different diameters. The only problem would be if the o-ring type were in fact influential in the opening force; then, they would have to run another experiment to disclose and separate the influence of material and diameter.

With that change, they would have a 25 full factorial design - five variables at two levels each. For a moment Mario thought, "I could run a fractional factorial here, but with so many non-believers, I better not push my luck."

At that point, Mario asked them if they concurred with the design and the experiment, and everyone agreed. It felt good, to help the group make a decision as a team, the Fuze team, instead of having them act like a bunch of tribal departments, all competing and accusing each other as if they were enemies.

"We're going to run the experiment tomorrow morning," Mario told them.

"Tomorrow is Saturday," said Bob, as he drew pictures of his new gadget to eliminate operator dependence.

"That's usually what comes after Friday, Bob," said Mario sarcastically.

"Okay, smart ass. Meeting is over for me," smiled Bob.

"Can you get that thing done for me today?" asked Mario.

"Not a problem. I'll have a fixture done today," Bob said with extreme confidence. "Do you need anything else from me?"

"No, that is it, Bob," Mario said. Bob was a great

designer and he could come up with designs as you were explaining problems during production. That had been Mario's experience with him. His visualization of words into things was incredible, but then Bob had been doing this for many years and was one of the main sources for most designs.

"Now I need a volunteer to get the piece parts we need from the warehouse," Mario raised his voice because everyone was talking to each other. It was funny, now all the accusations and disagreements were gone, forgotten or resolved. And all because they had finally managed to reach an agreement on what they were about to do.

Vicky responded, "I can get the piece parts, just give me a list of what they are."

Mario continued assigning tasks to most of the people in the room. He needed all of them involved in doing something related to the experiment. He wanted them to be part of the efforts so they would agree to continue working together later.

So far, Friday had been a hectic day, but luckily everyone had been responsive and cooperative at the end. Again, it felt as if they had formed a Fuze team; it was all of them against the evil that had caused the units to fail.

By six o'clock, they had everything organized to run the experiment the next day. Mario only needed a final word from Central Engineering.

The meeting broke up. Afterwards, he went upstairs

and as he found his way around the labyrinth of cubicles in the Central Engineering offices, Mario unintentionally eavesdropped on the young college engineer - he was explaining to Bob the factorial experiment they were running.

"Are you going to tell me he is going to run only two units in each of those cells and with that he is going to make a decision?" said Bob.

"No, Bob. He's making the decisions with all the units in the whole experiment, not just two," replied Dale with parental patience.

"But, why doesn't he run ten or twenty units on each cell? Two seems so few," Bob continued with exasperation.

"No, Bob. He's still using 64 units to make all decisions, not just two," Dale calmly replied.

"You don't understand," insisted Bob, "he's using two units here, and with that he's going to tell me if my fixture is good or not. That's totally unreliable."

The young engineer finally made Bob understand all 64 units were included in the calculation of each variable's effect. Bob, staring at the paper full of scribble, remarked, "That's pretty darn clever." Mario didn't intervene in the explanation because he knew Bob needed a design engineer-to-design engineer explanation to approve the method.

Bob had never had the exposure to applied statistics,

and he had never used experimental design before; he'd never had a reason to.

The business of Government contracts had always been protected by the nature of the contracts; that is, they had provided little or no incentive for efficiency and placed more emphasis on safety at any cost. Now, that was changing. Even though the company had come up with the design for the Fuze, they were not going to be the only supplier, there was going to be a second source. Competition was coming to Government contracts and that spelled EFFICIENCY, and efficiency implied the use of statistics.

The experiment took the whole day Saturday to run. It was a fun feeling for Mario, reminiscent of the overnight experiments. But from the current group accompanying him in this Saturday's experiment, the only ones that had taken part in some of the original overnight experiments were Vicky and Mark.

All during the day, people representing the different departments who attended the meeting had come, at one time or another, to see how things were going. Mario noticed some of them looked different in their casual weekend attire.

It was so late when they finished the experiment and collected all the data they decided to continue the tradition of going to the Salt Cellar Restaurant for dinner and drinks. There, they discussed the results and contemplated the data and plots. Throughout dinner and after drinks, they continued discussing and arguing, and challenging each other with what-ifs.

In those days they were still purists and fanatics when it came to statistics, and they would challenge themselves by doing all the computations with only paper, pencil and a calculator. It gave them the feeling they were really testing their abilities to solve a difficult puzzle. They thought software to analyze experiments was for wimps. The software at the time was all command driven and only used to double check results and produce the final reports. (Today's software and standard computer capabilities allow such computations to be done easily and quickly, even by non-experts.)

What they concluded, based on the data, was that the Assembly Technique appeared to be insignificant in its influence on the opening force of the units. The whole problem pointed in the direction of the design of the fuze and, mostly, on the selection of the materials used in the design: the o-ring material, diameter and lubricant. They knew the design people would not be too happy about this.

The o-ring material and diameter where intertwined and could not be separated. They were confounded as the o-ring type; Mario knew that from the very beginning. The o-ring type and the lubricant were both statistically significant, with a 99 percent level. They were also interacting and that interaction was also very significant. With these conclusions they had been able to account for over 87 percent of the variability in the opening force. That was remarkable, the experiment had been an undeniable success.

The o-ring type accounted for 76 percent of the vari-

ability and the lubricant for 6 percent, the rest was their interaction. So, if they could focus on the o-ring type they would
probably reduce most of the variability and improve the opening force, and have it not only meet customer specification limits, but probably exceed them with a Cpk of 2.18. In essence,
they would far exceed ± six sigma within the specification limits.

This meant they had achieved a solution to the problem
of the units opening at a high force. But what they had not
achieved was an answer to what had caused the problem. It was
definitely the o-ring type, but was it the o-ring material or the
o-ring diameter? They only knew it was a combination of those
two and, to a lesser degree, the lubricant. This implied they still
needed to continue with further experimentation.

On Monday morning, a full report of the experiment and
its findings was in everybody's in-basket, along with an invitation to an explanatory meeting.

As Mario had suspected, Bob, the senior design engineer, was quite displeased with the findings. The bottom line
was the Operator's Assembly Technique was not influential in
any way and the choice of o-rings and lubricant would potentially solve the problem.

The meeting lasted about two hours. During the meeting they proceeded to design the next logical experiment, which
would follow the direction pointed to by the current conclusions. In essence, it would have to include the most significant
variables: the o-ring material, diameter and lubricant.

"You're going to tell me that Assembly Technique bears no influence at all in the opening force? But you're telling me the o-ring and lubricant are the problem?" exclaimed Bob.

"That's exactly what the data is saying, Bob," Mario replied calmly.

"For crying out loud, these units are assembled by hand by operators, of course it should make a difference!" Bob cried out.

"Bob, the o-ring type and the lubricant are influential, no doubt. But we don't know if it's the diameter or the material or both. What we do know is the operators' technique has nothing to do with it," Mario asserted.

"I have trouble believing that!" said Bob with irritation. "I would like you to include the Assembly Technique again as a variable in this experiment."

"There is no need to do that," Mario started, "we have already proven it doesn't affect..."

"I hear you," Bob interrupted suddenly, "but that's where we disagree. I would be a very happy camper if you tried it again. If that's too much of a problem, I'll have my people do it."

"Bob, that will not be a problem. I shall include that variable in this experiment, once again," Mario assured him.

"Well, I have a problem with that," said Mark. "If we're going to try every insignificant factor all over again, we'll never finish."

"Let's not complicate matters and let's make this an exception," Mario stated with authority, as diplomatically as possible.

And so, the second experiment was planned and designed. This would be a 24 full factorial design - four variables at two levels each. But for this one, they would need to contact their o-ring supplier and get from them the right combinations of material and diameter, and that was going to take a few days.

For the next five weeks, the Fuze team bonded extremely well, running experiment after experiment to achieve the successful resolution of the problem of opening force, and successfully identifying what had caused the problem. Multiple statistically-designed experiments were planned, designed, conducted and analyzed to correct and optimize the Fuze.

As a matter of fact, over fourteen statistically-designed experiments were conducted by the Fuze team in a period of five weeks. Because of Bob's insistence and stubbornness, the first four experiments included the Assembly Technique factor. In all cases, the Assembly Technique was indisputably inconsequential upon the opening force.

It appeared the o-ring material selected originally was

not the ideal one for the application. It was a generic o-ring that included a compound which crystallized at a cold temperature, and this prevented the unit from opening at a lower force. The lubricant also played a significant role in increasing the variability and had a strong interaction with the material. The o-ring diameter had no role in the problem or solution.

Based on these final conclusions, they recommended the appropriate changes. And after a brief search, they found a better material and selected a more suitable lubricant.

The modified units passed the FAAT test with exceptional results and the Fuze program launched its Full Scale Production stage.

———————— • ————————

A coordinated and systematic investigation, focused on identifying causes based on valid data will always render better results if people work together in a spirit of true teamwork.

———————— • ————————

Smooth Transition from Design, FAAT to FSP

Personnel placed calls to all the Fuze program production operators and inspectors who had been sent home at the beginning of the shutdown. Most of them were waiting for the program to resume. They had already undergone special training and workmanship standards, and were certified operators and inspectors for a particular operation, and didn't want to go through all that all over again in another program. It was easier just to bite the bullet and wait.

As Mario walked into the production area that morning and looked around, he enjoyed seeing the production area full of people working as if it had never been shut down. People were walking in all directions, wearing the same white lab uniform. They were all familiar faces, and all very enthusiastic to go back to work at their stations, chartered with the task of going to Full Scale Production and having to deliver the products they had long trained for. The repetitious noise of the equipment gave Mario the sensation that at every click-clack a unit was being produced. It felt to him like the inside workings of a Swiss clock, as when all the pinions, gears and wheels start moving and time is produced.

"I knew you guys were going to come through," said Bill, as he walked by Mario.

Bill was a production operator who had been with the company for a lot of years and had seen this before. "Now the ball is in your court, Bill," Mario responded.

"Hey, won't let you down," Bill added.

Production started that same day and at the end of the day they counted 50 fuzes fully built, tested and packed. That was not bad for a good day's work!

In the next two months, production was brought up to 480 units per day, working only one shift. Second and third shifts were not allowed per contract; it had never been negotiated and, instead, a second source was to compete with the company.

During a period of five months, eight consecutive Lot Acceptance Tests (LAT) were conducted and all of them passed. Of all the units tested during the LAT's, only one single unit failed for a minor defect. Later on it was found it had failed only because one piece part had been out of tolerance -

the vendor's mistake - and it had been missed.

Even so, from the production of about 47,000 units, only one single unit had failed! It was unbelievable, not only to the customer, but to all of the people who worked there. All the previous work was all of a sudden worthwhile. All the animosities, the disputes and the egos were all pardoned and forgiven. The whole Fuze group, every single individual, became tolerant of each other as never before. Now they were a team again!

The customer had never experienced a weapons program that had started with the design of the product and had then failed its FAAT, only to recover from its failure. And not only had it recovered, but once in Full Scale Production, it had ramped up almost 1000 percent and completed the contract, delivering the product with only a single failure, and all within a single year. It was such an exemplary performance the customer sent a team to witness and report on what was going on.

During their visit a USAF Lieutenant asked Rob, the Quality Assurance and Fuze Program Manager, "What have you done differently on this program to make such a smooth and fast transition from design to Full Scale Production?"

"The major ingredient which is different from all other programs is the implementation of statistical methods from the beginning, and at each phase," Rob replied. "As a matter of fact, we have organized a presentation for you describing what we have done and how we have done it."

In the presentation Mario explained how all phases of product manufacturability (i.e., product design, equipment design specifications, machines, tooling, gauges, testers, assemblies, inspections and operations) thoroughly utilized statistical methods. The result was a production system capable of delivering excellent, defect-free product and of achieving a high-volume production output without jeopardizing quality.

All equipment, tooling and fixtures were carefully designed with a zero-defect approach. Design prints were carefully reviewed in brainstorming sessions. Risk and failure analysis was performed and potential problems were corrected to minimize design flaws during production. All machines, equipment and operations underwent carefully planned Process Characterization studies. Seventy percent of the machines (test equipment, tools, etc.) had a process capability index, Cpk, higher than 2.0 and the other thirty percent exceeded a Cpk of 1.0.

At the end of implementation, the manufacturing engineers were so convinced and accustomed to conducting Process Characterization studies - and it was so ingrained in their daily workload - that, on one occasion, one piece of production equipment underwent seven cycles of capability determination and optimization. After multiple modifications and redesigns of the equipment and after not achieving the results expected, it was considered unsuitable for production and it was scrapped, to be replaced with a brand new piece of equipment.

During production, minor problems arose but were aggressively corrected utilizing statistical methods. In the end, the final results were a first pass yield of 99.99621 or 37.8 parts-per-million defective.

The superior results achieved by Mario and all the teams also prompted other changes beneficial to the future of the Fuze program. Harry was promoted to VP of Manufacturing and moved to Central Engineering on the second floor, away from production. Ned, the Production Manager, was promoted in his place.

Now, with Ned as the Manufacturing Engineering Manager supervising all the manufacturing engineers, they were challenged to support production and to be fully committed to the implementation of the Process Characterization methodology, and to embark on achieving Six Sigma at each operation. Ned became a true believer of applied statistical methods; after all, he had participated in some of the overnight experiments and witnessed the results that Process Characterization could produce.

As for Mario, the success at the Fuze program led to a promotion and he skipped up two ranks in the engineering hierarchy to land at the same level as Rob, the Program Manager of the Fuze program. Needless to say, the program never again failed a LAT, and virtually all the product produced went directly to the customer defect-free - a true Six Sigma process.

_____ • _____

**The proof of any step-by-step methodology
is found not only in the results,**

but also in the level of acceptance throughout
the organization. The "buy-in" must be followed
by full integration of the "new" into the
"old" such that it becomes standard practice.

———————— • ————————

Optimizing the Administrative Process

The Fuze program had been running uninterrupted for five months now and operating at a very high rate of produc-. tion. Production was operating only on first shift as contracted from the beginning. The first-pass-yields were all at ninety-nine plus levels and production was running very smoothly.

The Six Sigma corporate program had started at the beginning of the year and was still being disseminated. It had been the driving force in initiating long-term studies in the Fuze program and, consequently, increasing the Cp and Cpk goals to 2.0. Ned, the new Manufacturing Manager, was very supportive of all that. He could not deny the Process Characterization program was responsible for the improvements realized in the Fuze program; he was a living witness and had been promoted due to its success. But the yields and the production quota appeared to have reached a plateau. He needed to concurrently increase the run rates of fuzes, to increase the current capacity, while maintaining the existing equipment and operating on one single shift. Operating on a single shift was a contractual clause the customer was unwilling to change. This constraint of only running one shift, coupled with the need to increase capacity, required further levels of optimization in the program. So Ned decided to call a meeting with Rob and Mario to discuss further improvements in the Fuze program.

"We are bound by the contract to only run one shift," Ned asserted looking firmly at Rob, as though expecting approval. "And we need to increase the run rates further from where we are now."

"We have cut down some of the time for inspection in a few operations by implementing new go/no-go gauges," responded Rob. "Also, we have asked the Test Equipment Engineers to combine some of the testing features to increase their speed in the functional tester."

"I know your people have been very supportive of the whole idea, but I'm afraid that's not going to be enough," said Ned in a very understanding tone of voice. Then, looking at Rob, as if trying to give him inspirational motivation, he exclaimed, "We need a breakthrough in the status quo! Something different from the normal."

"Well, Ned, I don't know what to tell you. We're trying our best to support manufacturing and I cannot require our inspectors to inspect any faster," said Rob.

"I have an idea of what we can do," Mario interrupted.

"Yes," said Rob as he turned to face Mario and looked him straight in the eyes.

"Let's hear it," said Ned, as if he knew all along Mario had an idea and was just waiting for him to say it.

For a moment, Mario thought Ned had invited him only to stir the pot. "Let's look at our process," Mario said enthusiastically.

"What do you mean? We already have people fully dedicated to doing Process Characterization studies. How much more can we do?" Rob asked, almost pleadingly, as if tired of the subject.

Ned was quiet, listening without twitching a muscle and giving Mario his undivided attention. Mario thought, "This guy is smarter than I suspected. This invitation was premeditated!" Ned had fed Mario just what he liked best - a challenge to improve things - and Mario could not resist.

"By our process, I mean, we, us, you and me, our departments, QA, manufacturing, the production staff," Mario added more enthused than before.

"What do you mean?" replied Rob.

"Let me explain," Mario said, "we, as a group, interact

with the production process with a lot of non-value-added operations and activities. Let's characterize these administrative
processes and apply the same tools and methods we applied to
the production process."

"I'm not too clear on this, but damn if I'm going to commit resources into activities outside the QA function!" Rob
complained.

"Rob, let me give you a few examples that belong to the
QA activity," Mario said respectfully. "We do 100 percent
inspection on all criticals. That QA activity slows the throughput."

"Well, 100 percent inspection is a contract requirement
and this program is under Weapon Specification standards, and
the customer is never going to change that," said Rob.

"Of course they're not going to change that. But we can
ask them to; especially, if we present them with an alternative,"
Mario replied flatly.

"What alternative could that be? The Weapon
Specification requires 100 percent inspection, period!" Rob
shot back.

"We have a process that runs at 99 plus first-pass-yield.
This is unheard of!" Mario said as he stood up. He continued
as if this were his only chance to convince them of what they
had in their hands, but did not realize. "What we have accomplished in this program, no other program or product in the

whole corporation comes even close to having. Even the customer admits it, and they're puzzled about what we did differently. They want the recipe. Now it's payback time."

"What are you saying?" Rob insisted.

"If we can sustain the yields and the quality - and I don't see what could prevent us from doing that - and we put a team together to thoroughly study the administrative process. And then, as an outcome of the study," Mario continued breathlessly, "we quantify and demonstrate the further improvements the Fuze program could obtain by going to a different inspection scheme rather than doing 100 percent inspection, I believe the customer would undoubtedly agree. Besides, high yields and high quality demand less inspection."

"First of all, sit down. Let's go slowly on this. Let's not get carried away," Rob said in a calm and controlling way. "This Fuze program is doing fine right now. It's meeting all production schedules. It's also meeting all print specifications, not to mention all quality and reliability requirements. At this rate we will finish the contract by year-end and on schedule. You're quite busy as it is, and there is nothing that's pushing us to do further improvements."

"Well, Rob, you know very well with this performance the customer may easily give us another contract on their next visit," Ned remarked. "Besides, the second source cannot even complete their pilot run yet."

Ned had insider information; he had gotten word of

another probable contract and that was his driving force.

"Rob, the improvements we've made so far in our production processes point to new opportunities elsewhere in our operation and the Six Sigma Corporate program says we should apply Six Sigma in everything we do. I think these are strong incentives for improving the administrative process," said Mario.

"Okay, tell me what could be an alternative to 100 percent inspection under the Weapon Specification?" asked Rob.

"There is a Military Standard 1235B for continuous sampling that can be applied or revised for our application. But that's not the issue, we can always design a plan. The issue is to look at the administrative process, characterize it, optimize it, and make it Six Sigma," Mario affirmed.

Ned immediately declared his support by saying, "Rob, I'm willing to go with his idea and I will provide all the resources for the team if you can spare him to guide us through the project."

"I'm concerned about Mario," said Rob. "He has too many things on his plate and, besides that, I see a lot of people from other programs coming to him for guidance and taking his time. He is supposed to spend 100 percent of his time on the Fuze program, but I know he spends 25 percent on other programs' charge accounts."

"Rob, most of the requests from other programs are just

incidental. They don't happen every month. Besides, this project will not take too much time. I would just be telling the team what to do," Mario lied through his teeth. He knew they didn't have a clue how to approach an administrative process, but he wanted Rob's approval.

"If he doesn't have a problem with it and you provide the people, I guess I don't have a problem with it, either..." Rob was saying.

"Okay! Let's do it," Mario said before Rob could finish his sentence and changed his mind.

"Make sure you get a charge number from Manufacturing to charge your time," Rob said as he stood up and passed by Mario on his way out of the conference room.

"Done deal," said Ned. "What do you need?"

"I would like Jay to be assigned to the team and between the two of us, we can set the core of the project. Then, later on, I will need two of your Process Characterization Technicians," said Mario.

"Okay, let's go at it one more time and let's see what we can improve. We should be able to shorten the cycle time somehow," Ned said as he adjourned the meeting.

Ned was all charged up. He had been in some of the overnight experiments and had faith Mario could find improvements and shorten the cycle time. Rob, on the other hand, was not too keen on making waves. He definitely did not see a need or reason to start changing something that was working fine. What he didn't see was there is always room for improvement, especially when the approach is proactive and the project is attacked with an open mind.

A big concern for Rob was the possibility of jeopardizing his wonderful performance as Fuze Program Manager by taking on such an unpopular project as eliminating 100 percent inspection on a Weapon Specification contract. His concerns were not unfounded. It was definitely a risky request, but Mario had no intentions of proposing anything not truly quantifiable and capable of improving the program with a high degree of confidence. Rob was the typical person who loved the milestones, but hated the journey.

Now, with the approval to move forward in making the administrative process more efficient, it was just a matter of treating it as a process and analyzing it using the same stage-approach as used in the Process Characterization studies done on the manufacturing processes. So the following day Mario met with Jay and they started to lay the foundation for the project. Mario knew Jay didn't know how to attack the characterization of the administrative process, but since Jay was the most open-minded manufacturing engineer there, that alone would help the project move forward.

After explaining the project to Jay, Mario said, "The first thing we should do is apply the same approach we used on our Rotor Assembly Process Characterization study."

"Wait a minute here, let me understand what they're asking us to do," interrupted Jay, with a look of confusion in his face. "They want us to improve the way we work?"

"Yes, but they want us to analyze the way we work and do some changes so as to improve the process and therefore, produce more product," explained Mario.

"What now, they want us to work like robots and speed up our work?" asked Jay.

"Not really, they just want us to work more efficiently," said Mario.

"Why don't they just yank up the conveyor speed! That will produce more product," Jay teased.

"No, Jay," Mario said laughing, "forget what I said. Let's take a totally different approach. In this Fuze program there are two sides that comprise the business. One side is the production process and the other side is the administrative process. Right?"

"I follow you."

Mario continued, "In the production process, we have people, machines, gauges, test equipment, fixture and tools. These are the things that comprise the process. The process also has a flow by which the products move from operation to operation."

"Okay."

"The production process has inputs and outputs and, through our studies, we make the process only produce good output by figuring out how to modify and set the inputs. That way, the process produces non-defective product, fast, at low cost, and very efficiently," Mario clarified.

"That's right."

"Well, now we need to do the same thing, but instead we concentrate on the other side of the business, the administrative process!" said Mario.

"I understand what you're saying, but what is this process. Everyone that comes to work does things differently and even if two people were doing the same work, they would still do it differently and they would change everyday. This is impossible!" Jay said.

"Wait, I don't think I'm expressing myself right. Let's look at an analogy," Mario replied.

"I'm all ears."

"When you wake up in the morning and you go to the bathroom to brush your teeth, what do you do? Describe it," asked Mario.

"Okay, first I get to the bathroom, then I look in the mirror and I say, 'You talking to me! You talking to me?'" Jay said jokingly.

"Okay, cut the crap, Jay," Mario said. "Come on, what do you do?"

"I grab the toothpaste, unscrew the lid and put it aside, then pickup the toothbrush and put paste on it and start brushing," Jay described.

"So, you hold the toothpaste without a lid on with one hand, as you brush with the other?" asked Mario.

"No, I put the paste aside. No, wait, I actually put the paste on the brush, place the toothbrush with paste aside, grab the lid, screw it on and put the toothpaste aside; then I brush my teeth," Jay tried to explain.

"So, just like that, totally dry, without any water? Like smearing peanut butter all over your teeth," Mario joked.

"Well no, I open the faucet, wet the toothbrush with the paste and then brush my teeth," Jay clarified.

"Do you close the faucet before you brush or do you leave the water running?" Mario continued.

"I leave the water running until I'm done."

"Why?" asked Mario.

"I don't know why, that's what I do. I guess I like the

sound it makes," said Jay.

"Wouldn't this process you just described be more efficient if you were to just wet the toothbrush then close the faucet and save water, instead of running water for no reason?" Mario said.

"Now that I look at it like this, I guess."

"I don't mean to spoil your morning routine, but this is exactly what we need to do. We need to find inefficiencies and speed up the execution of the process," explained Mario.

"So, tell me, when you wake up in the morning, how do you brush YOUR teeth," demanded Jay.

"I don't. First I eat breakfast, then I brush. Otherwise you have to brush twice, or end up spitting pieces of scrambled egg all over my face, like now," Mario jested.

"Oh, screw you!"

"Just kidding," laughed Mario.

"If we're going to have to analyze every job like that, it's going to be a lot of work," said Jay.

"Well, it doesn't have to be if we're efficient in our approach and only do it where it's necessary. First, we need to define the entities that make up the Administrative process. We have the QA organization, the Manufacturing organization, Test

Engineering, Materiel and Procurement, but we should just do QA and Manufacturing," stated Mario.

"I see."

"Then we will breakdown each organization into its members; such as QA Management, QA Engineers, QA Inspectors, etcetera," Mario said. "Then we will define what their different activities are; for example, the QA Engineers interpret the customer prints and define and write all inspection instructions, set sampling plans, disposition product and design gauges, etcetera. The QA Inspectors inspect the units produced at each operation based on the inspection instructions and do that according to the sampling plan; in our case, 100 percent of the product. I think it's here where we can start making the administrative process better."

"Yes, there are possible errors, mistakes and inefficien-cies all along the way. So, if you write a really crappy inspection instruction, then this would make the inspectors make mistakes and misinterpret the product quality requirements," Jay continued sarcastically.

"That is funny, Jay," Mario agreed. "So as you can see, there are a lot of things we can potentially make more efficient and error-proof."

"The 100 percent inspection is another area where we can improve. That's pretty inefficient," Jay remarked.

"Well, that's the one I brought up in the meeting with

Rob and Ned yesterday, and Rob was very reluctant to even talk about it," said Mario.

"Why?"

"Because it's a contract requirement. But I'm pretty sure we could change that," Mario affirmed.

"Then let's go ahead and do it!" Jay said eagerly.

"Don't worry, we will get to it. But first, we need to analyze the administrative process in an unbiased way. That is, regardless of where we suspect we can get benefits, let's allow the data to tell us where the opportunities for gross improvements lie," Mario said.

"Okay, I think I get the idea of what we need to do," said Jay.

By the end of the day they had dissected the whole administrative process and had pulled a few people to assist them in other parts of the organization in which they had better understanding. By the end of the week, Mario, Jay and the others had a complete decomposable map of the organization - with inputs, outputs and how they interact with each other and with the production process. It gave them a macro and a micro view of who, what, where, and when the work was done. With that portion done, they moved into the measurement generation stage and to distinguish who the internal and external customers were and how to recognize their needs, wants and requirements.

"Since I've been working in industry, there has always been this adversarial relationship between Quality Assurance and Manufacturing, and the funny thing is both service the same customer," Mario said to Jay and to Freddy and Wayne, the Process Characterization technicians who joined the team during the week. "Since we're already here, each of us representing one of these organizations, let's define the customers for each organization."

"Well, the US Government is our customer," said Freddy.

"Yes, but we have more than just one customer. We have the US Air Force, Navy and Marines. These are three different customers," said Jay.

"You're right Jay, but those are the ones that buy our products. How about the internal customers, the ones for whom we do our daily work?" said Mario.

"You mean, like who do we do our Assembly Instructions for?" Jay asked.

"That's right. When you design and write an Assembly Instruction for operation 925, who is your customer?" Mario asked back.

"Well, that would be the operator at 925," answered Jay.

"Equally, when we design an Inspection Instruction, our customer is not only the QA inspector but also the production people for that operation. In essence, the service QA provides is borrowing the units produced by the operator and using their judgment and the Inspection Instruction, and making an unbiased decision on whether the unit is good or bad. So, for Quality Assurance, the customer is also the Production Organization," Mario said.

"Yes, but the Production Organization reports to Ned so, then, QA's customer is, after all, Manufacturing," said Jay, laughing.

"That's purely circumstantial. Don't look at it that way. Imagine the Production Organization reports to a manager at the same level as Ned and Rob. Then, QA and Manufacturing service the Production Organization," Mario reiterated.

"Okay, I guess," Jay acknowledged.

"Better yet, reflect on this: the Production Process is the heart of the business. It produces the product we sell to be in business. That gives us employment. If we allow the Production Process to get a heart attack - like the one we had when we failed the FAAT - we run the chance of loosing our jobs." Mario declared.

"You're right!" exclaimed Jay.

"Now, what does the heart do? It distributes blood to the rest of the system," remarked Mario.

"So, when you guys don't feed it too much cholesterol,

the Production Process distributes a paycheck to every employee," said Freddy. "And how ironic, at the end of the day, I find both of you serve me!"

"Hey, that's pretty funny, Freddy," said Jay feeling uncomfortable. "This is getting too philosophical for me, man."

"Okay, okay. What we need to do is define our internal customers for the major activities we do, and then figure out a way to interview those customers and listen to what is important to them. Then, we should transform that information into the response variables we would need to optimize," Mario said.

After spending the rest of the meeting devising ways to gather information and opinions from internal customers without being too obvious, they concluded the two process technicians were the best way to maintain secrecy. Once they gathered and processed the information, the results were fascinating.

"So, Freddy, what did you get for me?" Mario asked at their next meeting.

"Well, we're almost finished with the majority of the operations. Wayne and I covered one operator from each operation and we kind of recruited Vicky to talk to the inspectors. No matter what kind of form and method we used, the strongest message is time, time, time. It takes too long to do this, it takes too long to do that. Also, paperwork is a major issue to everybody. It's too difficult, it takes too much time to fill out and it's very easy to make mistakes," said Freddy.

"How about cost?" asked Mario. "Are there any statements or entries under cost?"

"This is funny, but not a single person made any references to cost, except the Production Manager. Everybody is hung up on time and the difficulty of the paperwork." Freddy said.

As they further defined the information gathered, the team decided to concentrate on three main responses: time, paperwork and opportunities for errors. The time was defined as the elapsed time to produce and inspect a unit; the paperwork included the Travelers, Inspection and Assembly instructions; and the opportunities for errors were the number of chances for committing errors and mistakes.

Mario and Jay had the process technicians concentrate on data collection and information gathering to quantify the status of their administrative process. As they analyzed all the data and determined their performance, cycle time, throughput and PPM, they were shocked by the potential for further improvements. The outcome of the Performance Determination stage clearly defined for them areas to concentrate on; areas that, upon streamlining, they were sure would maximize product output, paperwork reduction and error and mistake-proofing.

Mario and Jay continued working with the two process technicians, Freddy and Wayne. The four of them had regular meetings every day to analyze results and identify and assign action items, concentrating only on the three responses.

"Freddy, how are you coming along with your data collection at the Transducer Assembly operation?" Mario asked.

"I spent about an hour collecting the time to produce and the time to inspect a unit. It takes an operator an average of 40 seconds to produce a sub-assembly and about 15 seconds for the inspector to inspect it. There are nine points of inspection in that operation," Freddy rattled.

"What was your sample size?" asked Jay, wanting to make sure Freddy had used a number representative of the process cycle time.

"I took about sixty readings, measuring different operators and inspectors at different times during the day, so the data is not biased," replied Freddy. "I also made sure they didn't catch me doing it."

"Pretty good, Freddy," Mario said. Freddy had been trained very well and his experience in gathering data and information was making him a necessary asset to the program. He had gone from a shy operator, to an assertive but still humble process technician.

"So this operation also confirms inspection takes about an additional 38 percent of the production time," Mario added.

"For the almost ten operations I have finished, the average is now about 35 percent of production time," said Freddy.

"It has come down a bit," Mario said.

"Well, yes. I think, so far, we can say inspection takes an additional 35 percent of production time," repeated Freddy.

"Wow!" exclaimed Jay. "That's a pretty significant amount of time sucked up by a non-value added operation."

"Well, Jay, it's not so non-value added when it assures the customer we can build to print. Besides, so far, it's a requirement," Mario said.

"How about if we have the operators do the inspection of the units and eliminate the QA inspectors altogether?" Jay remarked.

"You cannot have the same person doing the work, inspect their own work for quality. That simply will not fly in any government contract," stated Mario.

"Well how about if the next operator checks the work of the previous one? Then, they would not be inspecting their own work," Jay said.

"That could work, but it could never replace QA inspection," Mario said.

"So you're saying we cannot eliminate 100 percent inspection?" asked Jay.

"Not entirely," responded Mario. "But let me tell you what I'm thinking we could do. Imagine this: What if we establish a Kanban system in which the operations work on a pull system of manufacture? Operators verify the work done by the previous operators, so they don't add more work to units that may be rejected, or fail to meet the quality. That way, operators assist by being fully aware of quality requirements. At the beginning of the day, we bring a Screening crew, made up of QA inspectors, to qualify the process by doing 100 percent inspection for a predetermined time. If no defective units are found, they qualify the process and 100 percent inspection stops. Now we bring a Checking crew, again made up of QA inspectors, but this time they only do random sampling inspection instead of looking at every single unit."

"Hey, that's a great idea!" exclaimed Freddy.

"So, instead of inspecting 100 percent of the units we produce, we could be inspecting about 30 percent of the whole production," said Mario.

"What if a unit fails?" asked Jay.

"Well, if a unit fails, depending on which mode we're in, Screening or Checking, we would have to investigate and qualify the process all over again," responded Mario.

"You mean, do 100 percent inspection again?" asked Jay.

"You bet! If the process is running well and we're randomly inspecting, finding a defect in a unit implies a degradation in the process, so we would have to stop it, do corrective action and requalify the process and bring the Screening crew back for 100 percent inspection. If we find a defect during the qualification, then we're screwed! That means the process is not performing to the expected quality level. So again, we would have to stop the process for manufacturing to improve," Mario noted.

"If the process continues performing the way it's now, we would do really well with this kind of inspection," said Freddy

"Of course, almost 70 percent of the units we're inspecting now, would not be inspected at all, and that could add an additional 120 units to production," proclaimed Mario.

"We could be heroes if we get this done," said Freddy.

"Freddy, how about the other data you're collecting on the travelers?" requested Mario.

"Oh, that. Yes, it's also very interesting. I've found the travelers are taking about 10 percent of production personnel's time and there are a lot of places where they're making mistakes in the paperwork," Freddy indicated.

"We could change the production to a paper-less system using bar-codes, but that's more difficult to justify for improvement, the numbers are not there," said Jay, pretty disappointed.

"I think once we improve the inspection methods, the paper-less numbers would be the place to obtain the next highest improvement and, at that point, they will go for it. Right now, the best ROI is on the alternative to 100 percent inspection," Mario said, as Freddy and Jay gave him signs of approval.

A month later, a Continuous Sampling Plan using the MIL-STD-1235B was designed and approved by Rob and Ned and presented to the Headquarters Armament Division, Deputy for Munitions and Armament Equipment for consideration to replace 100 percent inspection. After a few modifications, it was approved and implemented in the Fuze program.

It turned out they had underestimated the improvements to the program. Instead of 70 percent of the units not going through 100 percent inspection, they found, upon implementation, it was actually 81 percent. This increased the throughput and reduced the cycle time significantly. A few months later, the production process changed to a paper-less system with the implementation of a bar-code system and the total elimination of the Travelers. At the end of the third quarter of 1987, the Fuze program was the most innovative program in the organization. And by year end, the profitability of the program was a record 136 million dollars.

——————— • ———————

**Optimization must be achieved at all
process levels. The focus of all such activity**

must be the identification and elimination of non-value-added operations in the complete process. Only then can throughput be increased, cycle times reduced, costs lowered and profit potential maximized.

———— • ————

Six Sigma in Everything We Do by 1992

Immediately following the Christmas and New Year's holiday in 1986, the CEO delivered what was to be one of the most influential and transforming speeches in the Corporation's history. To be more exact, it was on the morning of Thursday, January 15, 1987, that the speech was communicated by video to all the employees, over one hundred thousand spread over six continents. The Six Sigma Quality Program was launched.

By eight forty-five in the morning, people started arriving in the cafeteria for the communication meeting. As they slowly focused their attention on the television sets which had been temporarily hung at two extremes of one side of the cafeteria, most people were still talking excitedly about how they had spent their Christmas holidays. But when the CEO appeared on the color screens, the buzzing of the crowd quieted down to listen:

"I'm using this extraordinary medium to communicate with each one of you because I want to secure your immediate dedication to a new level of quality performance in our organization.

I want you to understand that by improving the service we offer each and every one of our clients, we can all realize and benefit from an increase in the number and frequency of orders we will receive.

I know these are difficult times and our orders are relatively weak; but I also know we could improve them by 5 to 20 percent, and thus achieve greater stability in our business, if we could just rise to the occasion and meet or exceed our clients' needs in both our products and our services.

How do I know this? Because during the last few months I've been visiting our clients, and what I heard directly from them was both encouraging and challenging. All of them emphasized how much they liked our products and working with our organization - and that was encouraging.

But then, too, they all mentioned we could stand to improve our service; they stated their dissatisfaction with things like filling, delivering, documenting and billing of orders. Apparently, we could stand to be more thorough and accurate in these areas.

However, they also said they would be willing to

increase their orders to us by 5 to 20 percent if we could just satisfy these kinds of needs - and that was the challenge.

So we have been working hard to come up with a new plan to improve our quality into the future. And we have arrived at what we think will help us make the necessary improvements. So let us not waste any more time and let us bring all of our processes and procedures and, in fact, everything we do to the highest level of excellence so we can meet our long-term goals.

However, if we want this to be a good year and we want it to be profitable, we will need to do more. We will need to jump right on it and address our clients' needs immediately. In essence, we will need to meet or exceed the level of excellence our clients expect in the next three months.

And we can do it! We've got to do whatever it takes to meet or exceed our clients' expectations in the short term and make it appear to them that we offer them not only the best product, but the best service, as well. If we can do this, I assure you we will increase our orders and we will start seeing the positive effects in the next four to nine months.

If, however, we fail to convince our clients we're the best in both our products and our service by the end of this first quarter, I assure you we can expect to lose many of our hard-earned clients to the competition.

For this reason, I will be working with our Corporate Management to produce an executive directive that will further clarify the goals and initiatives that will help us achieve the necessary excellence to meet or exceed our clients' expectations in the next three months.

And I will be communicating with all our Managers and Supervisors to ensure they understand how important it is that they wholeheartedly embrace the responsibility of leading the deployment and implementation of these initiatives.

But for now, I want you to pay special attention to our new corporate quality goal. I've made sure there is a copy for each and every one of you, so please take one, read it and commit to it, because I and every single member of our Committee on Policy have approved it and committed to it - and we expect all of you to fully embrace it and commit to it, as well.

I know we all try to do the best we can and we often give it our all, but we must also understand there is always room for improvement - always. So, I'm telling you that from now on we must strive to surpass our clients' and even our own expectations. I'm telling you that we need to excel in the eyes of our clients and our own. I too will need to excel in everything I do, every single day, in the eyes of our clients, yours and my own. If I can do it, you can do it - and if you can do it, I can do it. So, let me repeat myself: if we're to succeed, we must meet and exceed our clients' expectations in everything we do for them.

I ask you to join me and commit to our new goal, and to get involved and make implementing this program and achieving the objectives, your top priority."

The speech was very energetic and motivating, and most people spent a great deal of time reflecting upon what was said. Immediately after that, they were presented with the revised Corporate Quality goal, and it incorporated a very aggressive rate of improvement and the Six Sigma Quality goal. The goals were as follow:

- Improve product and service quality tenfold by 1989.

- Improve product and service quality one-hundredfold by 1991.

- Achieve Six Sigma performance capability by 1992.

The message strongly requested of every employee, with a deep sense of urgency, a dedication to quality in every aspect of the organization. It carried the overall objective of achieving a culture of continuous improvement and ingraining it in every aspect of they daily work, so they could perpetually provide total customer satisfaction. And it asked them to do this nonstop, until the ultimate goal of zero defects was attained in everything they did. It went even further by asking and insisting everyone prepare for perfection in all their endeavors with their customers, and that every employee function should be perceived as serving the customer.

Furthermore, everyone would be responsible for the goal and equally responsible to each other with respect to the goal. And, finally, it emphasized no one could assume to have done enough until the entire goal were achieved throughout the whole organization, at a corporate-wide level.

The message was crystal clear. It unequivocally stated, "Achieve Six Sigma performance capability by 1992, in everything you do."

For the next few weeks there was a lot of discussion within the organization about what the employees were expected to do to achieve the new corporate goal. The most confusing issue was the meaning of Six Sigma; particularly, because it took Corporate two weeks after the CEO's video presentation to publish a description of what the Six Sigma Quality Program was all about. The document was called "The Six Sigma Challenge" and it was divided into two explanations: What is Six Sigma? and Why Six Sigma? It was only one page.

The following Tuesday Mario arrived very early to work. His usual routine was to go to the front offices, where the secretary for the engineering area was stationed, and pick up his incoming mail. That particular day there was not much, just a one-page document printed on 60-pound card-stock entitled "The Six Sigma Challenge." There was no accompanying letter or distribution list. It didn't even say who it came from, it was just the document and it was in everyone's mail box.

Due to Mario's curiosity on the subject, he devoured the document and reread it three times while sitting at the secretary's empty desk. As people were trickling into work, they could not pass the opportunity to make smart remarks when they saw him sitting in the secretary's chair: "Finally, you got promoted" or "I liked the other secretary better." Mario just smiled as he continued reading. Then he got up and walked back to his cubicle. When Mario got there, Rob, Ned, Jay, a couple of other engineers and Eddy - the Ayatollah of Process Controla, still working with another program - were already discussing and interpreting what the document had failed to clearly explain.

"Have you read this?" asked Jay holding the document in his right hand and waiving it up and down.

"I just came from picking it up and read it three times already. It is kind of confusing, isn't it?" Mario replied.

"That's an understatement!" answered Jay.

"You're the local guru, so we're coming to you for an explanation," said Ned.

"I like my steaks medium well; I could not be a guru," Mario kidded. "Eddy looks more like a guru to me!"

Smiling, everyone looked at Eddy. Then Ned interrupted, "Take a few minutes to read this again. I would like to ask you a few questions, Mario."

"Yes," agreed Rob. "I also need a few clarifications on some numbers."

"I wanted to talk about this document, too," added

Eddy.

"Why don't we all go to the conference room so we can use the blackboard," suggested Rob.

"Great, I'll meet you guys there in a few minutes. I'm going to get some reference books," Mario said as he grabbed some statistics books and searched quickly for the tables in the appendix.

They all left for the conference room and they continued discussing the document. As Mario walked towards the conference room, he noticed they were still commenting and arguing outside the room.

Ned opened the door and found two people inside. He said, politely, "Hi, could you guys continue your meeting in my office? We're a bunch and we can't fit there."

"Sure," one of them replied; and they quietly put their things together and left.

They all sat around one side of the room and Mario interrupted their on-going discussion by saying, "Let's start from the very beginning of the document, paragraph by paragraph, so we're all in tune here. So go ahead, everybody read the first paragraph and then I'll go through it."

As they all finished reading the first paragraph, Mario said, "It says, 'What is Six Sigma?' and it's supposed to give us the definition of Six Sigma but, instead, it just reiterates Six

Sigma is the required capability level to approach zero defects. And the new standard is now zero defects and the goal is to be best-in-class in product, sales and services. As to the goal, I don't think there is any doubt or that we need to discuss it further. The company's expressed initiative is the achievement of error-free performance in providing products and services to its customers. But error-free output is a matter that would require and demand full attention to detail at all levels. It also requires a strong and clear understanding of how our customers view satisfying their needs. We're talking about design, procurement, production and management in the organization."

"We don't have a problem with that section," said Rob.

"Wait a minute," cautioned Eddy, "that's supposed to be an explanation of what Six Sigma is, and all it says is that it's our goal. What about an explanation of what it really is?"

"Well, yes, you're right, Eddy. It doesn't explain what Six Sigma really is, but it's in the next section where it's covered," Mario indicated.

Ned was more anxious to get to the section he had troubles with, so he insisted, "Come on, let's go to the next section!"

"Okay, this next section is about 'Why Six Sigma?' although it also covers a little of what it is. The explanation describes the performance of a product by how much margin exists between the design requirements, in other words, the specification or tolerance of its characteristics, and the actual value of those characteristics. And that is regardless of whether those characteristics were produced at our factories or at the factories of our suppliers," Mario described.

"So, what is that in layman's terms?" asked Eddy.

"In layman's terms, they're saying products have characteristics - those are the things we measure. And they also have specifications for those characteristics - and those are what our customers want us to produce to. So the performance of our process is measured by how well we can produce against those specifications," explained Mario.

"Go on," said Ned.

"It further asserts that each process attempts to reproduce its characteristics identically from unit-to-unit, but some processes have more variation than others. And, because most characteristics follow the Normal distribution, that variation would be measured in standard deviations from the mean," Mario said.

"Wait right there," said Ned, "what do they mean by saying that most characteristics follow the Normal distribution?"

"Yeah, we have a bunch of characteristics in the production floor that we know don't follow the Normal distribution," said Jay.

"Well, you guys are right. There are characteristics that

don't follow the Normal or Gaussian distribution, but you have to understand they can be approximated fairly close and, at worst, all we would be dealing with is just an over or underestimation in our results. That's no big deal. There are ways to deal with that statistically," Mario maintained.

"Okay, great, continue," said Ned, satisfied with Mario's explanation.

"And then it says the standard measurement of a process width is computed as ± 3 sigma about the mean," Mario continued.

"Please go ahead and explain what you just said," interrupted Ned.

"The process width refers to how much variation the actual manufacturing process has when producing a particular product or, in this case, one characteristic on a product. For example, if your characteristic is supposed to be .020 inches and you're over or under that value when producing it, then your process has variation when producing this product's characteristic," Mario conveyed. "Now, this variation is the process width, and it can be quantified by calculating the standard deviation or sigma. As a matter of fact, the sigma is the unit of measure to quantify variation. Once we have the value of sigma, we multiply it by six (plus or minus three equals six) and that becomes the standard measure for process width."

"What do you mean by standard measure?" asked Eddy.

"The standard measure is the common way, the regular way, the academic way of calculating variation. This is the way we have always calculated it and the way it will always be calculated until eternity. This is like 2 times 2 equals 4. When did it start and when will it end? This holds true forever," proclaimed Mario.

"So, to determine the process width or variation of any process, all I do is multiply six times the standard deviation? Period!" Ned exclaimed as he slapped his open hand against the table.

"You got it," Mario said. "That is cast in stone. Nobody changes that."

"And how do we get the standard deviation, again?" asked Ned.

At this point, everybody started laughing.

"You ask Mario, he'll give it to you," remarked Jay laughing.

"No, you get your calculator and press the random number generator. It will give it to you," said Eddy.

"You can do that if you're desperate, but the right way is to collect a bunch of data and, using the formula for the standard deviation, calculate it," Mario interceded.

"Okay, good, let's continue because in the next paragraph I have a bunch of questions," Ned said.

Mario continued, "Then it says that approximately 2700 parts per million will fall outside the normal variation of the ± 3 sigma process width and, although this may not appear to be disconcerting at first, it becomes very detrimental to the rolled yield as more parts are used in building a product."

"Where are they getting this 2700 parts per million?" asked Rob.

"When you consider a product with a characteristic that is normally distributed or Gaussian, the measurement of its process width is ± 3 sigma or ± 3 standard deviations. In the Normal distribution, ± 3 sigma encompasses about 99.73 percent of the distribution, that means that 0.27 percent would remain outside the ±3 sigma limits. Now imagine the specification for this characteristic is such that it coincides with the ±3 sigma limits, this would imply we produce 99.73 percent of our product for this characteristic within specification and, in effect, 0.27 percent would be outside or defective." Then Mario restated, "So, if we produce a million products, 2700 would have this particular characteristic outside the specification, and we'd consider them defective."

"But we're never going to produce a million Fuzes, why should we worry about such a small percentage?" questioned Jay.

"I know, but just imagine what will happen when we do produce 47,000 fuzes: we will have 127 failing on that characteristic alone," stressed Mario.

"Well, that's not so bad," said Rob.

"Yes, but we're not dealing with only one characteristic in our fuzes. The problem gets compounded as we have more characteristics. Just imagine, in one operation we're inspecting over nine characteristics and in the complete Fuze we have hundreds of characteristics and that doesn't even include all the characteristics at the piece-part level!" Mario cautioned.

"Yes, you're right," interrupted Ned.

"Imagine this. Our first contract was for 47,000 fuzes; now consider, for the sake of argument, one hundred characteristics - although we have more than that. If for these one hundred characteristics the process performs with a quality level where only 0.27 percent are outside the specification limits and 99.73 percent are good, we would still have the potential of having 11,134 fuzes with a defective characteristic and only 35,865 defect-free," Mario said.

"Well, now it doesn't sound so good, Rob," mocked Ned.

"Now I would like to know, could you sleep at night knowing that inside the arsenal you have 11,134 fuzes with characteristics out-of-tolerance? Especially, when not knowing whether those characteristics could be on the detonator safety lock or not?" queried Mario.

"So then, why are they talking about parts per million, if we don't produce millions?" asked Eddy.

"For a couple of reasons. One is because, although we may not be producing a million finished products in our processes, we may still have more than one million characteristics going through our processes," clarified Mario.

"That could be so, but not in our industry," added Rob.

"Come on, I'm referring to our production area," said Mario.

"How so?" insisted Rob.

"Come on Rob! In the Wave Solder area we solder printed circuit boards in panels. Each board has an average of 56 components and there are four boards per panel. That's roughly about 224 joints," recited Mario. "Most boards are plated-through-hole boards, so both sides are inspected for defects; that's a conservative 448 per panel. Four boards go to each fuze and our contract was for 47,000 fuzes."

"That's 21 million inspections!" exclaimed Eddy, as he finished punching the numbers in his calculator.

"And that's only if we inspect one type of defect, like insufficient solder," added Mario.

"I know. They inspect for more than twelve different kinds of defect categories," said Rob.

"And they do that in a split second. I don't think you can get a robot that can inspect faster and for more characteristics simultaneously than the human brain," Mario said.

"Maybe we should love our inspectors a little bit more," replied Rob.

"Yeah, Rob. Maybe you should take them out for pizza," snapped Eddy.

"Okay guys, let's cut the crap and continue. This is the part you were all experts on before," interrupted Ned.

"Wait, wait! What was the second reason, Mario?" asked Eddy.

"Well, the other reason is that you want to consider using 7 or more decimals when measuring the performance of your process, because it's at a level that the numbers are changing," Mario said.

"Okay guys, let's continue. I don't want to be here all day," said Ned.

"Then the next paragraph concludes, 'Thus, we can see that for a product to be built virtually defect-free, it must be designed to accept characteristics which are significantly more than ±3 sigma away from the mean.'" Mario read.

"Not a problem, continue," cried Ned.

So Mario continued, "'It can be shown, then, that a design which can accept twice the normal variation of the process, or ±6 sigma, can be expected to have no more than 3.4 parts-per-million defective for each characteristic, even if the process mean were to shift by as much as plus or minus 1.5 sigma.'"

"Finally, you got to it. This is the most confusing thing in the whole damn document!" Ned screamed, releasing his frustration.

"Where are they getting these numbers?" asked Rob.

"Okay. First let's reread the first sentence in the document and hold it in our minds; the goal, that is. Now, in the previous sentence they're implying if you design a product which has a specification or tolerance significantly bigger than the size of your ±3 sigma process variation, the product could be virtually defect-free. In other words, if you have a specification or tolerance for a characteristic and it's bigger than the size of your ±3 sigma process width - and imagine the specification with respect to your ±3 sigma is getting larger and larger and now it's almost twice as large - then the product produced would be getting closer and closer to defect-free," Mario said.

"Yes, I could agree on that for the time being," said Eddy.

"Well, it makes sense. If our process has less variation than the specification or tolerance, then all the product would be defect-free," agreed Ned.

"Yes, they're saying if it was significantly larger than ±3 sigma then, of course, the larger the better. I would tend to agree with that," said Rob.

"Now, in the next paragraph they're saying, if the tolerance was as much as double the process width of ±3 sigma, in other words ±6 sigma, then, of course it would be definitely better. Right?" Mario asked.

"Right!" said everybody.

"Great! So, we all agree on that?" said Mario.

"Wait! Why double and why not less than double?" asked Jay.

"Well, that takes us back to the original goal which I asked you to keep fresh in you mind. The goal is to approach the standard of zero defects and be best-in-class. So, what ratio of tolerance to process width takes us closer to zero defects?" Mario asked rhetorically. Continuing, he said, "That would be twice; in other words, the specification or tolerance has to be twice as wide as the process variability. If we look at a Normal distribution table and identify a value of Z for ±6, which is double our process width, we would have about 99.9999998 probability of product within the tolerance. In essence, this implies that almost 0.0000002 percent of the product or 0.002 PPM would be outside the tolerance and would have defects. Granted, this is not zero defects but it is very close to perfection. It's only 2 defective per billion produced!"

"Yeah, but it's still not zero defects," contended Jay.

"Whether or not 100 percent perfection can be achieved and sustained is something we can argue until hell freezes over; but one thing is true, making our process width be one half of our tolerances is something we can undoubtedly achieve," Mario declared.

"But why would we want to go to such extremes in quality?" asked Ned.

"Come on Ned, we've done that and even exceeded that in many of our operations. It doesn't take much to reduce the standard deviation value in half. You have witnessed how we've done that with experiments," said Mario.

"Yes, you're right." agreed Ned.

"It's not as fantastic as it sounds. Let me give you an analogy. Have you heard of all the problems we had with the Gag Rods in the Rotor Assembly operation."

"What are you talking about? We never had any problems with the Gag Rods - not from day one!" answered Ned.

"The only reason you didn't hear of any problems with the Gag Rods is because, from the very beginning of this program, all the characteristics of the Gag Rod were made with process widths which were one half or less of their tolerances.

They were already made to perfection. They were already Six Sigma. Otherwise you would have heard about it being a problem and we would have had to fix it," Mario said.

"What are you trying to say?" asked Ned.

"Very clear. Everything in our process you haven't heard of as being a problem, is most likely because it was already far over or close to Six Sigma. That's why you didn't hear about it in the first place," Mario said. "We, as engineers, don't concentrate our efforts on the good things; we mostly concentrate our efforts on the bad things, the ones that give us problems - the ones that are not yet at Six Sigma."

"So, you're saying if every characteristic were made to be Six Sigma, our processes would produce nearly perfect product and we wouldn't hear of any problems?" asked Ned.

"You got it!" Mario exclaimed. "Now, Ned, let me ask you a question, because I've never understood the logic of this. Although it may apply more to Harry, when he was managing the Fuze production."

"Okay, Mario shoot," Ned replied.

"In the case of the Gag Rod, we know those characteristics are already beyond Six Sigma. Why should those characteristics be allowed to be Six Sigma or higher, and the ones we have problems with, the ones that surface as problems everyday, you guys object bringing them to the same level as the Gag Rod? Why that double standard in quality?" Mario asked.

"Well, we've become complacent and we just want to produce product, but we don't want anything to stop the momentum. I guess we get addicted with the production rush and we simply deny the process has any problems, and we sacrifice it with a quick fix," said Ned.

"Thanks, that's the best explanation I've ever heard," Mario said.

"What about this 3.4 PPM level? Where's that number coming from?" asked Eddy.

"That's a bit tricky. For that you have to analyze the sentence very carefully," cautioned Mario.

"Okay, do it," said Eddy.

"If we have a product with a characteristic whose specification is twice its process width of ±3 sigma, it means we would have about 99.9999998 percent within specification and 0.0000002 percent outside the specification. This would undoubtedly be a process that produces almost perfect product," Mario asserted.

"Okay, I follow you," said Eddy.

"Now, imagine that for some unforeseen reason, one of the characteristics were to shift by a significant amount - the document refers to this as, even if the process were to shift. The question to you is: Would a 0.01 sigma shift in the average be a significant shift?" asked Mario.

"Most likely not," replied Eddy.

"How about 0.6 sigma; would that be a significant shift?" Mario said.

"Well, maybe not; that's only a 10 percent shift," said Eddy.

"So, for all practical purposes, let's assume 1.5 sigma is a significant shift in the average; as a matter of fact, that's one fourth of the process width, or a 25 percent shift. That would definitely be a significant shift," Mario asserted.

"That would be a significant change! We would definitely hear about this shift. It would be more like drop everything you're doing and work on this!" said Jay sarcastically.

"What they're trying to tell us is even if the process were to shift by as much as 1.5 sigma, we would still be okay with this process because we could still guarantee our customers this significant shift would not be a detriment to our product's quality and, at worst, it would produce only 3.4 units-per-million defective," Mario explained.

"Let me repeat what I'm understanding. So, what they're saying is our processes and their products have in essence a warranty. Since our products would be produced by processes which are Six Sigma, not even under unsuspected significant shifts would the customer see a detriment in their quality. Because, at worst, their defect level would be 3.4 parts-per-million," Ned recited with pleasure at his full comprehension.

"So with Six Sigma, what is the defect level we're shooting for?" asked Eddy.

"Go back and reflect on the first sentence of the document. The goal is Six Sigma capability to approach zero defects. Six Sigma gives us a goal yield of 99.9999998 percent or a defect level of 0.0000002 percent, or about 0.002 parts-per-million defective. Now, that's pretty close to zero defects," Mario said.

"Where are they getting then this 3.4 parts-per-million number?" inquired Eddy.

"If you have improved your process and now its' process width is one half of the tolerance, you have made it ± Six Sigma. Now, if this distribution were to shift because somebody screwed up and that shift were a significant one, such as 1.5 sigma, then you would no longer have your distribution in the center of your specification limits. It would be shifted to one side, increasing the probability of having defects by the closeness to that spec limit, and your defect level would increase from 0.002 PPM to 3.4 PPM. Look at the Normal distribution table for a Z of 4.5 sigma and take one half because it's shifted. That will actually give you 3.45 PPM," Mario said, as he started showing him the calculations on the black board.

"That's right," said Ned. "All they're saying is shoot for making your processes ±Six Sigma and then if the unforeseeable happens, such as a significant 1.5 sigma shift in the mean, the customer will not be affected by it. So, buy our products, the competition doesn't provide that safety warranty."

"Hey, that's a great marketing slogan!" said Rob.

"Yes, but now we need to provide that safety warranty in our processes by making the process widths one half of the current specifications," said Mario.

"So, that's 'The Six Sigma Challenge,' to make every process for every characteristic be Six Sigma or half the current specification, even though these specifications were not designed to accept twice the process width," said Rob.

"I interpreted it as if we were allowed to have a 1.5 sigma shift in our processes from now on," said Jay

"Not in your dreams, Jay," Mario replied.

"Okay, so where are we? Is that it?" asked Ned impatiently - he wanted to leave.

"Then, the document continues with the formulas of Cp and Cpk to show the 1.5 sigma shift," said Mario.

"We already understand all that. We have seen it many times," said Ned.

"That's it, then," Mario said. "The rest just reiterates the goal is a five year goal to achieve ± Six Sigma capability in products, sales and services."

"This whole document just tells us the goal is this, the goal is that, but where does it tell us what the hell we need to do to achieve this goal? Where is the recipe we're supposed to follow?" asked Jay.

"Jay, are you trying to say here, 'Where's the beef?'" Mario said with a grin on his face.

"Well, we've been following Mario's interpretation and methodology all along and, don't get me wrong, this has been great because we're ahead of everybody and leading the whole corporation, but are they going to give us an approach?" insisted Jay.

"I sincerely think they will. They'll probably come up with another document like this, telling us what to do," said Rob.

"Because I can just see somebody saying, 'Hey, let's open our specs to double the tolerance and we will get to Six Sigma in a split second, not this five year crap.'" said Jay.

"That wouldn't work anyway, Jay," Mario said.

"What better approach are you waiting for, Jay? We've been applying the Process Characterization methodology and, so far, it's been infallible. We've tried it with all our processes and every time it's brought them to Six Sigma capability or beyond," replied Ned.

The meeting adjourned and Rob, Ned, Eddy and Jay had a better understanding of The Six Sigma Challenge. In June of 1987 the document was revised and the goal statement changed to "Six Sigma is our Five Year Goal to approach the standard of zero defects in everything we do."

For over a year and two months, after the inception of the Six Sigma Quality program on Thursday, January 15, 1987, there was no recipe to follow but the Process Characterization methodology. Finally, in March of 1988, Corporate published the Six Steps to Achieve Six Sigma, which applies only to administrative processes and is totally inadequate for technical processes.

———————— • ————————

**The real challenge in the achievement of
Six Sigma not only encompasses total commitment
in everything we do, but also the use of a clear, concise and
understandable step-by-step
methodology to make such achievement both feasible and
attainable for everyone in the organization.**

———————— • ————————

No, Not Again!

In August of 1987, after a very hectic year and after spending countless hours at work with the Fuze program, Mario decided to take a nice two week holiday in England and Greece. After spending a civilized week in London visiting all the tourist spots, Mario flew to Athens to spend a week on the beautiful island of Skiathos. That is where Greeks go for their holidays when they just want to relax on a beautiful island beach, away from the tourists.

Two years earlier, Neil Winderhoff graduated with honors from a reputable university in Boston, Massachusetts. He had gone all the way with his education and graduated with a Doctorate in Statistics. Immediately after his graduation, he found a position with the Semiconductor side of the same organization Mario worked for.

Now, on a Saturday morning in 1987, Neil woke up feeling pretty content with his life and accomplishments. He thought, "There are only a few people that have a PhD degree, and I'm one of them." In the last few months Neil had made two major purchases, he had bought a house and a brand new car. He was only 34 years old and had never been married and now he had a wonderful job and a very rewarding salary. In the two years spent in Arizona, he had made a lot of friends; and, although most of his friends were not colleagues at work, his girlfriend was. He was very much in love and sincerely considering asking her to marry.

He had spent the whole past week in a classroom, training all the operators from the Metalization areas of all three Wafer Fabs. And it had not been easy because of their lack of a statistical background. It had not been easy for him to teach Statistical Process Control to operators, but that was part of the change needed at that facility. He had grouped the operators by area of responsibility instead of mixing their functions and had placed them in small groups of ten so they would not feel intimidated. First he trained the engineers and now, to finish, he needed to cover all the operators, a very time consuming effort. By the end of the week he was physically and mentally exhausted but, that morning, his feeling of accomplishment was at an all time high.

Neil had spent the last eight months implementing control charts in the Wafer Fabs. His efforts in implementing control charts in the Fabs lead him to make numerous presentations to customers and potential customers who came to either audit or tour the production areas. After one of these presentations, a customer showed a strong interest in getting his employees trained by Neil, and the unsolicited offer of remuneration had whet Neil's appetite. Although he was in no serious need to supplement his pay, it was definitely an enticing excuse to do it. So he agreed to spend the whole following week with this customer, training his production operators and technicians. This commitment made his weekend unusually short for he had to fly to Michigan, early on Sunday.

Looking out at the blue and sunny sky from the second floor of his house, he thought, "Sunny Arizona, what a great place to live!" He didn't miss the cold, miserable winters in Massachusetts, and that triggered the thought of taking his girlfriend on a ride in his new red convertible Alfa Romeo.

He spent his whole Saturday with his girlfriend and decided to retire early because Sunday was going to be a very tedious day. It was going to be a pack-and-fly day, so he made arrangements to be picked up very early, so he would arrive at the airport on time.

The airport was not as busy as usual, that Sunday. The early morning flight was not popular with most weekend commuters, but he liked the idea of leaving early because this was going to be his first engagement to do training outside work.

During the next following days he delivered the now familiar training package he had been delivering at work. The only problem he experienced with his new audience was all his classroom exercises were related to semiconductor technology.

His audience was mostly involved in electronics assembly and he lacked the experience in these processes. Luckily, his audience was not the inquisitive kind and did not ask too many questions during his presentation, so it was smooth sailing. And at the end, the comments from his audience were very positive and management was very happy with him.

Every night, he telephoned his girlfriend to tell her every detail of what happened in the classroom. He could not believe how much money he was getting paid for doing this. This was the most profitable vacation he had ever taken.

Friday came quicker than expected. Teaching everyday made the week go fast and because he had no time to visit any place, he decided to stay the weekend and visit some college friends in Ann Arbor. So he called his girlfriend to tell her he was staying the weekend and had changed his reservations to take the last flight on Sunday, en route to Phoenix...

Mario waited patiently with more than one hundred other people to take the ferry. After spending a very relaxing week sunbathing on the beaches of Mandraki, in the Bay of Xerxes, island of Skiathos, Mario was going home. The ferry took all of them from the lively main port, back to Agios Konstandinos on the mainland, and from there Mario took a bus to Athens. The following day he arrived at the airport early and boarded the flight that took him back to London. The flight was uneventful and once he arrived at Gatwick, Mario took the train to Heathrow; he would depart from there to the United States and had plenty of time to spare.

As Mario passed a newsstand he was astonished as he stared in terror at the headlines of an English paper that read, "Phoenix-bound Flight from Detroit Crashes, 152 Dead." It was shocking, especially since he had been away overseas for only two weeks. Mario felt very sad for all the people on that unfortunate flight and hoped there was no one aboard he knew. Overall, it was not a pleasant feeling for Mario at the airport that day. Especially since he was ready to take a long transatlantic flight back to the US. And, in fact, upon his arrival in Phoenix, Mario was glad to learn there had been nobody he knew on that flight.

In the first week of November, Mario received notice the Semiconductor organization was looking for somebody to coordinate the implementation of Six Sigma for the US and all its' worldwide operations. Being unbelievably interested in such a challenge, Mario sent his curriculum vitae. Not too long after that, Mario received a strange telephone call giving him only the time and location of the interview, and the name of the interviewer. Mario was told by a female voice he had only thirty minutes and the interview would be conducted by the Vice President of the Semiconductor organization. She ended the call by saying, "Be on time."

The interview came sooner than expected, and Mario didn't feel quite prepared for it. He knew his chances were limited, given the constraint of only thirty minutes. "Thirty minutes," he mused, "eighteen hundred seconds. It takes five seconds just to say my name, and if he doesn't get it, it takes another five to repeat it. I'm down to 1790 seconds already! And how do I address him? Mister Vice President?" Too many silly things were going through his mind.

Mario arrived with plenty of time. He waited in the adjacent room to the VP's office, with the secretary. Her name was Julie. She proceeded to brief Mario on a few things. "His name is Charles and he's a very busy man, so you will have to stick to your thirty minutes. He never allocates that much time, not even for his staff," she said, in an assertive but pleasant way. "You're a very lucky young man. He's giving you that much time, so use it appropriately. Don't waste it, go straight to the point; he likes that."

Mario was starting to show signs of being worried and she immediately reassured me, "Oh, don't you worry. Charles is sweet, kind, and a gentleman. You'll do just fine." As she talked to Mario she kept typing on her word processor and answering incoming calls. Mario was surprised she had not announced him, but since there was plenty of time he decided to obtain some information about the position. To his questions, all she disclosed was there had been seven other individuals interviewed, and Mario was the last one.

"This is very unusual, you know, because the seven people applied for the job. On the other hand, he asked me to call you," Julie said.

"Oh, so you were the one who called me about the job opening?" Mario asked.

"Of course, who did you think it was?" said Julie.

"Well, I didn't know. You never gave me the chance to ask. You just gave me the information, asked me for my Mail Stop and ended the conversation rather quickly," said Mario.

"Oh, believe me, I would have liked to chat more, but I just follow instructions around here," Julie claimed.

"So, he asked you to call me?" Mario asked.

"You know, I used to work for the Government side of the business, too. It was great! 7:15 to 3:45 and you were out of there. You still had the whole day to yourself. But then they started reducing head count and I came here. You know, it's more stable here. I've been working for Charles for twelve years now," Julie confided.

"So, how did he hear about me?" Mario inquired.

"He has friends in high places, you know," Julie replied.

"I don't doubt that but, come on, you probably know everything that goes on here," Mario said.

"You better believe it! Okay, but don't mention it to Charles," Julie whispered.

"I promise," Mario whispered back.

"Charles' organization supplies components to the program you work for, you know. And, two weeks ago, two people from there came to have a meeting with Charles. They bragged about how well they were doing and how they were awarded the CEO Quality Award. Then your name came up," Julie said.

"I wonder who they were?" Mario asked.

"Well, you can wonder all you want, because that I won't tell you! Have you forgotten of the 'need-to-know' young man? I haven't and that you don't have the need to know," she stressed. "Wait! It's time. I need to tell Charles you're here." And dropping everything she was doing, she continued thinking out loud, "If I don't break up their meeting, they're going to suck up all your time. They always do that - make no appointment and just take his time and interrupt the whole schedule." She stood up, walked fast with small steps to Charles' door, knocked once and opened quickly before giving anybody the chance to answer. Then, very politely, she said, "Excuse me, Mario is here waiting for you." They exchanged a few words and then she closed the door abruptly, and turning to Mario, she said, "It'll only be a minute now. But remember what I told you: he's very busy, so manage your time."

At that moment, the door opened and three individuals came out. All very well dressed. Mario stood up and froze, not knowing who to address and just waited with his eyes dancing from face to face, waiting for and expecting a gesture that would give away which one of the three he should approach first. Mario didn't want to introduce himself to the wrong person - that could be quite embarrassing - and those few seconds felt like minutes. That's when Mario realized how nervous he was.

It was then that a fourth person came out and walked directly to Mario with a secure and gentle walk and, extending his right hand, said, "You must be Mario. I'm Charles. Come on in and sit down."

They went through formal but cordial introductions and then Charles proceeded, "My organization is scattered all over Phoenix and we're finishing a new Wafer Fab in Malaysia. We interface with plants all over Asia-Pacific on design, assembly, packaging and test. We also have subcontracting houses that also do assembly for us, and we have suppliers here in the US and overseas. For the last few years, we have concentrated heavily on Control Charts and we have four years left to achieve Six Sigma. I know you have been very successful in improving the Fuze program, but that's in one location. We, on the other hand, are scattered over continents. I want to bring all these sites towards Six Sigma. How would you go about doing it?" As he finished, he rested comfortably in his chair and gave me his undivided attention.

"We're going to need to train all of these people on how to achieve Six Sigma. I'm currently writing a book on a methodology to achieve Six Sigma and we could use it for training and fast dissemination. Then, we should standardize this methodology across the whole organization, so it's applied consistently at every single location and we don't have people reinventing the wheel. What I've learned from implementing this in the Fuze program is most people don't know what to do or where to start to make their processes Six Sigma. They need to see an example that shows them before and after, and shows them all the details, every step they need to take to make it Six Sigma. It cannot be broad or macro. It has to be very detailed, micro, and put forth in a very systematic way, step by step. Once they see this, they won't have a problem following it," Mario said.

"How would you get it implemented?" asked Charles.

"It has to be from the top down. We would have to start with upper management, then their staff, and then down to the engineers, and finally operators. We would do that here in the US, as well as in every other single site overseas," Mario said.

"So, are you telling me you're going to train me and my staff, as well?" Charles questioned.

"Of course! How else can I convince all your people you guys are serious about this, but by training you and your staff? Besides, I need to convince you control charts are not the starting point if you want to achieve Six Sigma," Mario declared.

"What do you mean?" demanded Charles.

"That's the last thing we did in the Fuze program. The first thing in characterizing a process is defining it, so we can understand it, so we can eventually control it. Not the other way around," Mario clarified.

"What happens after training the management?" Charles inquired.

"Once we have their commitment, then we will train their people in teams with specific processes already assigned to them. If management cannot show its commitment, we should not provide any training until they are fully committed," Mario said.

"Why is that?" Charles asked.

"Because if the individual site management is not committed, eventually nothing will be accomplished. The people are not going to spend their time doing studies their management doesn't see as a real priority. At the end of the day, the people only work on what they're asked to work on. So from upper management to their immediate supervisors, they have to demonstrate this is one of the things they want accomplished," said Mario.

"Don't worry about that. My people are very committed to this and if they don't show you their commitment, that's where I come in to help you. You just have to let me know who they are," Charlie said.

"Absolutely. Now, you want every site en route to Six Sigma, right?" asked Mario.

"That's exactly what I'm looking for. I want every person, process and product on its way towards Six Sigma, and I want them to sing the same song everywhere," Charles affirmed.

"Well, the Six Sigma program is very clear in its objective and goals. It talks about achieving Six Sigma by 1992 in everything we do. So, it's here we need to start classifying all the things we need to bring to Six Sigma. Every process in a site has to be brought to Six Sigma; every product every site produces has to be brought up to Six Sigma. Every machine, equipment and tooling has to be raised to Six Sigma and eventually every department and job function. This implies we will need to establish the order of priority in our efforts to do this by 1992," Mario stated. "So one of the tasks I will impose on the site management will be to establish this order. I will guide them through a workshop to classify all their processes and steps according to their criticality in providing total customer satisfaction. This, in essence, establishes the order by which the teams are going to study their processes over the next four years to bring them to Six Sigma."

"That's exactly what I'm looking for! I want everybody, every process and every product to be impacted. Otherwise, they get complacent and we don't improve," Charles exclaimed.

"Absolutely, that's what Six Sigma is all about. If we just apply it to a product here and there, and a process here and there, then it's just problem-solving and eventually it turns into fire-fighting," Mario said.

"Believe me, we're masters at that already. We have made it an art around here," Charles noted. "Well, everything you're telling me is just great. Go on."

"With the processes classified, we can then establish a Four Year Plan for Six Sigma by scheduling and categorizing all the processes into critical, major and minor. According to that hierarchy, we schedule them over the next four years and we define the number of teams we need and the team members. By then, the whole site knows exactly what processes are going to be improved, by when and by whom - and the whole Six Sigma plan is established. This way, there are no surprises; nobody questions the seriousness of the commitment by management and how we manage and track the Six Sigma program," Mario explained.

"What if the site management is not willing to go through this exercise?" Charles asked.

"That's exactly how you determine if the site management is committed or not. If they have no sincere intentions of bringing their process to Six Sigma, they won't want to spend their precious time making a detailed four-year plan, when they don't intend to support it or when they don't expect it to still be active in the third or fourth year. This exercise reveals their true faith in the Six Sigma vision," Mario said.

"How would you track improvement?" Charles continued to cross-examine Mario.

"There are going to be multiple ways in which we will do that. Let me just explain a couple. First, at the detail level, the studies will be divided into five stages, which is how the methodology is divided. We will then track each team and study by their completion of each stage. At each stage there are deliverables the team has to provide. These deliverables ensure the stage has been completed and they're not skipping or taking shortcuts. These deliverables also become part of the documentation of the studies, which helps keep them for posterity. By the completion of the five stages, the process will be at Six Sigma and we will have archived the recipe to keep it at those levels. The only way to finish a study is by finishing the five stages in progression and that implies achieving Six Sigma. So we will be tracking scheduled versus actual for each stage and team," Mario said. "The second way has to do with setting up Six Sigma Performance Indices at each site. These indices will be tracked during operations review, every month, against quarterly and yearly goals, and all the way to Six Sigma by the year 1992."

"What would be a typical Six Sigma Performance Index?" Charles asked.

"There are certain things that improve inherently as a process moves towards Six Sigma. One of them is scrap, which should go down. If it doesn't, but the team claims the process has been brought to Six Sigma, there is a disconnect somewhere, and we should suspect shortcuts. The process will need to be audited by an outsider, possibly me. Other indices are first-pass-yield, part-per-million defective, Cpk, customer returns, on-time delivery, etcetera. Besides that, we could track other indices that may be of interest to you. We will probably have to identify projects and focus on improvements for those particular indices," Mario said.

"We will probably want to improve cycle time, on-time

delivery and customer returns," Charles said, as they heard a knock at the door quickly followed by the door opening just enough for Julie to step through.

"David wants to know if you're going to have a meeting with him. He has a customer meeting to attend. What should I tell him?" asked Julie.

"Tell him that I will be busy the whole morning and schedule him for tomorrow," Charles replied.

"Two thirty in the afternoon?" Julie suggested.

"Perfect," said Charles.

"You want a coffee break? I just finished making a fresh pot of coffee," said Julie.

"Would you like a cup of coffee?" asked Charles.

"Thank you, that would be nice," said Mario.

"Make it two cups, Julie," Charles said politely.

"Mario, how would you like your coffee?" asked Julie.

"Just black, thank you," Mario said. Then Julie closed the door and Charles asked Mario questions about his personal life and interests. A few minutes later Julie came back with the coffees and the interview resumed.

"I think you have a clear idea of what needs to be done. What would you need to make it happen?" asked Charles with genuine interest.

"I will need to have some people reporting to me directly. Statisticians would be preferable. But if you don't have them, I'll train them. I will need about four people," Mario requested, hiding his excitement.

"I could give you three people and an open requisition. Currently, I've three people who have been involved in the implementation of control charts. They're not statisticians, but they're very good. What else?" Charles asked.

"We would need to establish a formal Statistical Methods department, with me at the head," Mario said.

"That won't be a problem. You want to make it official?" Charles said, surprising Mario.

"That's right. This department would report directly to you," Mario suggested.

"Wouldn't it be more appropriate for it to report to my Quality Assurance organization?" Charles asked.

"That would be a disaster!" Mario exclaimed.

"What do you mean?" asked Charles.

"Well, right now I work in the Quality Assurance side of

the Fuze program, and it's a perpetual struggle to deal with manufacturing. If the Statistical Methods department were under QA, we would be a typical quality organization, telling manufacturing they need to add quality to their production activity - as if there were two ingredients in a product. Quality and all the tools of Six Sigma should be skills in the manufacturing organization and belong in manufacturing. But this Statistical Methods department cannot report to the manufacturing organization, because it would be restricted and its efforts would be sacrificed to the fluctuation of quantity in production. Having this department report directly to the Vice President of the organization demonstrates no other motive but the commitment to increase the quality, efficiency and performance of the whole organization to Six Sigma. This department should be totally unbiased. Its charter should be to educate, disseminate and manage the implementation of statistical methods to achieve Six Sigma by 1992," Mario articulated his vision.

"What about after 1992?" asked Charles.

"By then I will have either succeeded or failed," smiled Mario.

"Now, tell me a little more about this methodology to achieve Six Sigma. Is that what you implemented in the Fuze program?" Charles inquired.

"Well, not exactly. This is a bit more than that. In the Fuze program, management was not entirely committed. So I had to push it from the bottom up. And believe me, that's for the birds! It gets really old very quickly. What I've been putting together is how to drive it from the top of the organization, as it should be. I've been incorporating a lot of the lessons I've learned," Mario affirmed.

Now the interview continued more as a conversation between new friends than a real interview, and lasted two hours before Mario left Charles' office.

"Mario, it was a pleasure talking with you. I will be in touch with you, probably within a couple of weeks. If not, Julie will call you. If you want to check the status, please call Julie; I may be traveling the next two weeks," Charles said. Then he simply went back into his office and closed the door.

So Mario turned to Julie and asked her for her telephone number. She gave it to him and said, "Don't worry, I'll get in touch with you as soon as he makes a decision. I have your number."

"But he's going to be traveling pretty soon," added Mario, a bit worried.

"Don't worry, you did great! None of the other seven ever finished their thirty minutes. I told you, he's too busy. Believe me, you did fine," she reassured Mario.

"Really?" asked Mario.

"Two hours! Get out of here," she said with a smile.

Mario was feeling pretty good as he left the office.

Three weeks later, as Mario arrived at his cubicle in the morning, the phone rang before he could sit down. It was Charles. "Congratulations! When can you officially start?" he asked.

"I could start immediately," Mario said with enthusiasm, "but I probably need to give my boss a two week notice."

"I'll call him; give me his number. I need the Head of the Statistical Methods department on board soon! I got you everything you asked," Charles announced.

Mario could not believe it! He had been made the Head of the Statistical Methods department, reporting directly to the Vice President of the Semiconductor organization. His charter was to disseminate and implement Six Sigma throughout the whole Semiconductor organization in the US and overseas. When he hung up the phone, Mario screamed so loud that everybody stuck their head out of their cubicles. Mario, on the other hand, remained sitting down trying to contain his excitement.

A week later Mario spent his first day at the Semiconductor organization and two days later he found out, to his astonishment, he had once again replaced an individual who had passed away. That individual was Neil Winderhoff; he had been one of the 152 passengers on that unfortunate flight from Detroit to Phoenix.

——————— • ———————

Achievement of Six Sigma requires a process-focused methodology that is top-down-driven. Success relies on incorporating training, standardization, prioritization, quantifiable expectations, performance measurements and continuous comparative assessment. All must be done with a preannounced time-frame to achieve a predetermined organizational goal.

——————— • ———————

Six Sigma
Part II

Understanding the Concept, Implications and Challenges

I. Introduction

What is Six Sigma?

Six Sigma is many things: a statistic, a metric, a strategy, a goal, a benchmark, a vision, and a philosophy. Some have even incorrectly supposed or implied Six Sigma to be a methodology. So many possibilities have inevitably lead to much indecision and confusion about Six Sigma. For this reason, it is helpful to define and clarify the true meaning of Six Sigma.

Six Sigma is an optimized level of performance approaching zero-defects in a process producing a product, service or transaction. It indicates achievement and maintenance of world-class performance. Six Sigma is not a methodology. It is an end not a means.

A good starting point to explain Six Sigma might be to

start first with an explanation of what sigma is.

II. Understanding Six Sigma

What is Sigma?

Sigma is a Greek letter, σ, used in mathematical statistics to represent the standard deviation of a distribution. In mathematical statistics, letters symbolized in Greek are used to represent parameters, and their values are always unknown. So, the value of sigma is always unknown, but it is estimated by calculating the standard deviation from a representative sample.

The theoretical Normal (or Gaussian) distribution has two parameters, the mean, μ, and the sigma, σ. Since, the mean and the sigma are represented with Greek letters it implies their values are always unknown, but they are estimated by calculating the average and the standard deviation. The average and the standard deviation are two statistics that are computed from samples to estimate the mean and sigma.

So sigma, or for all practical purpose, the standard deviation, is a statistic that quantifies the amount of variability or non-uniformity existing in a process, response or characteristic. In effect, sigma and standard deviation are synonymous.

Sigma is a measure of the amount of variability that exists when we measure something. In the case of a product, we usually have many characteristics important or critical to quality. We usually collect data and measure the sigma of some of these characteristics. If the sigma value is large it tells us there is a lot of variability in the product. If the sigma value is small, then the product has very little variability and thus, very uniform. We are always attempting to produce uniform product with hardly any variability. So, the smaller the value of sigma, the better the characteristic, product or process. How is sigma computed or estimated? For more information, please refer to "Frequently Asked Questions", (FAQ's) in part III.

$$S = \sqrt{\frac{\sum_{i=1}^{n}(X_i - \overline{X})^2}{n - 1}}$$

Six Sigma is Many Things

As indicated before, Six Sigma means many things, and it is used in different ways, sometimes causing a bit of complexity for the newcomer. Here are a few definitions that might help you understand the subject:

Six Sigma the Benchmark. Six Sigma is used as a benchmark to compare the quality level of processes, operations, products, characteristics, equipment, machines, divisions, and departments, to name a few.

Six Sigma the Goal. Six Sigma is also a quality goal. The goal of Six Sigma is to get very close to zero defects, mistakes or errors. But it is not necessarily zero, it is actually 0.002 parts-per-million defective, 0.002 defects per million, 0.002 errors per million, 0.002 ppm, or for all practical purposes zero. It is not 3.4 parts-per-million defective, as is often mistakenly cited by some.

Six Sigma the Metric. Six Sigma is a metric for a particular quality level. When the number of sigmas is low, such as when referring to a Two Sigma process, implying plus or minus two sigmas ($\pm 2\sigma$) within specification, the quality level is not so good. The number of defects or defectives in such a process may be too high. As compared to a Four Sigma process, ($\pm 4\sigma$), where we may have plus or minus four sigmas within specification, the quality level might be significantly better. So, the greater the number of sigmas within specification, the better the quality level.

Six Sigma the Philosophy. Six Sigma is a philosophy of perpetual improvement of the process (machine, manpower, method, metrology, materials, environment) and reduction of its variability in the never-ending pursuit of zero-defects.

Six Sigma the Statistic. Six Sigma is a statistic calculated for each characteristic critical-to-quality to assess performance to the specification or tolerance.

Six Sigma the Strategy. Six Sigma is a strategy based on the interrelationship that exists between product design, manufacturing, delivered quality and reliability, cycle time, inventories, rework, scrap and defects, as well as mistakes in everything done in the process of delivery of a product to a customer and the degree to which they influence customer satisfaction.

$$\pm 6\sigma = 12 \cdot \sigma$$

Six Sigma the Value. Six Sigma is a composite value derived from the multiplication of 12 times a given value of sigma. Assuming 6 times the sigma value within specification limits to the left of the mean and 6 times the sigma value within specification limits to the right of the mean in a Normal distribution. Failure to understand the implications of this is at the core of many of the misperceptions and misunderstandings surrounding Six Sigma as will be made clear later.

Six Sigma the Vision. Six Sigma is a vision of taking an organization to a status of best-in-class. It is an intrepid crusade to go after variation, defects, errors and mistake reduction It is extending quality beyond customer expectations. By providing more, customers want to buy more, versus having sales people coaxing and persuading customers to buy.

Six Sigma before January 15, 1987

Before, January 15, 1987, six sigma was understood by academia, and by the rest of the world, as plus or minus three sigma within specification limits.

To illustrate this, imagine there is a particular characteristic being measured in a process. Imagine the process builds computer keyboards, and the characteristic of importance is the force to depress a key. Let's call this characteristic the Key Tension Force. Such a characteristic has a design specification. If the force required is too high, it would take to much force from the user to strike a key. If the force required is too low, just by resting a finger on the key might produce a keystroke. The design specification has then an upper specification limit, USL, and a lower specification limit, LSL. Realistically, when these limits are exceeded, the product has failed its design requirements.

Later on, as we build a quantity of keyboards and test them, we collect data, compute the sigma and predict the process variability or what is also referred to as the process width. In our particular example of computer keyboards, the process variability is only related (or attributed) to one characteristic, the Key Tension Force. And although we might make reference to process variability, we distinctively mean the variability in the amount of tension-force needed to produce a keystroke.

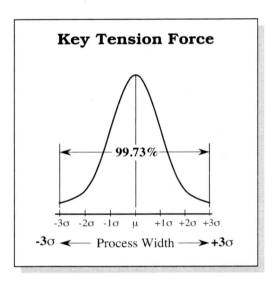

The process variability, or process width, by convention is always measured by multiplying 6 times its sigma, that is, the sigma of the characteristic. This formula never changes! Why six? Because in a normal distribution the area under the curve between plus or minus three sigma (±3σ) encompasses or includes about 99.73% of the distribution. And although 99.73% does not encompass the entire (100%) of the distribution, it is for all practical purposes close enough to be considered all. So, when we compute the process variability we have included almost all, but accept the result as if it were all.

Academia understood six sigma to signify that process variability (±3σ) was equal to the distance between the upper specification limit and the lower specification limit.

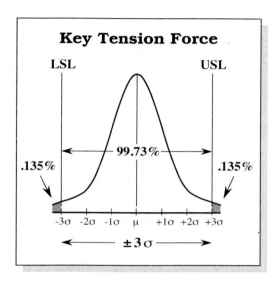

Under this definition a six sigma process was understood to be a process with plus or minus three sigma limits within specification limits. Such a process would have a Cp of 1.0 and if the average was centered in the middle of the specification limits, then, it would also have a Cpk equal to 1.0. A process with a Cp and a Cpk equal to one, would then have about 99.73% of its product within specification and about 0.27% out of specification, or 2,700 ppm. As can be seen, none of these numbers agree with what is today understood as Six Sigma. Why is that? Because on Thursday, January 15, 1987,

Motorola Inc., launched their "Six Sigma Quality Program", and that changed how six sigma would be understood from then forward.

Motorola's Six Sigma Quality Program

On Thursday, January 15, 1987, Motorola Inc., launched a long term quality program they called "The Six Sigma Quality Program". The program was launched by Bob Galvin, Chief Executive Officer of Motorola, Inc., with a speech that was distributed throughout his organization in writing and on videotape. The video was distributed to every sector, group and division Vice President and General Manager and viewed by the GM's staff, which was later viewed by their staff, thereby cascading throughout the organization comprised of about ninety-nine thousand people around the world in about 53 major facilities.

In his speech, Mr. Galvin explained that for the previous six months he had, with some frequency, visited many customers and although they had mentioned they liked doing business with Motorola, they also expressed a desire to be better served. They wanted better service in delivery, order completeness, accuracy in records on each transaction, etc. They further suggested, if they would be served better, with total quality emphasis, Motorola could expect from 5% to 20% more business from them·in the future. Mr. Galvin, suggested company employees rise to the challenge and offer the customer the expected level of quality service, and that it be done with a deep sense of urgency.

Additionally, Mr. Galvin took the opportunity to emphasize to management their special role and responsibility to lead the implementation of this program. He stated the Corporate Quality Goal had been updated to include this new challenge.

Finally, Mr. Galvin accepted the challenge himself, by saying: "I must do my job perfectly in the execution of each daily detail as observed by the customer." and he challenged everyone by saying: "You must move to the same objective."

Six Sigma after January 15, 1987

The program was a corporate program which established Six Sigma as the required capability level to approach the standard of zero-defects. This new standard of zero-defects was to be done in everything, that is, in products, process, services and administration.

The Corporate Policy Committee of Motorola, then updated the Quality Goal as follows:

"Improve product and services quality ten times by 1989, and at least one hundred fold by 1991. Achieve Six Sigma capability by 1992. With a deep sense of urgency, spread dedication to quality to every facet of the corporation, and achieve a culture of continual improvement to assure Total Customer Satisfaction. There is only one ultimate goal: zero-defects - in everything we do."

The revised Corporate Quality Goal committed to the achievement of total customer satisfaction now. In other words, Motorola would be the best in all products and services as perceived by each customer by March 31, 1987. In effect it directed every employee to prepare for, and insist on perfection in all dealings with the customer. Everybody's function was to be interpreted as serving the customer. The revised Corporate Quality Goal stated that everyone was responsible for and to each other regarding this objective. Finally, it affirmed that no one could assume he or she had done enough until the entire goal of Six Sigma was achieved company-wide. The revised Corporate Quality Goal was then signed by:

Bob Galvin, Chairman,
Bill Weisz, Vice Chairman,
John Mitchell, President,
George Fisher, Deputy to Chief Executive Office,
Gary Tooker, Chief Corporate Staff Officer,
Jack Germain, Motorola Director of Quality,
Jim Lincicome, Government Electronics Group,
Carl Lindholm, International Operations,
Levy Katzir, New Enterprises,
Jim Norlin, Semiconductor Products Sector,
Steve Levy, Japanese Operations,
Don Jones, Chief Financial Officer,
Jim Donnelly, Personnel,
Ray Farmer, Communications Sector,
Ed Staiano, General Systems Group, and
Gerhard Schulmeyer, Automotive & Industrial
    Electronics Group.

From my personal experience with some of these individuals, I can say they not only signed the document, they also talked the talk, and walked the walk.

The "Six Sigma Quality Program" was defined at two levels. First, at the managerial level; every individual of the organization was responsible for their process, product and service and challenged to characterize it and improve its quality to six sigma performance levels, thus, bringing total customer satisfaction. Second, at the operational level; it required the use of statistical methods to characterize technical (manufacturing) processes by means of metrics such as Cp, Cpk, sigmas, and to characterize as well, non-technical (administrative, service or transactional) processes by means of ppm, dpu and other metrics.

The purpose of the "Six Sigma Quality Program" was to improve customer satisfaction or what they internally called "Total Customer Satisfaction" (TCS) by reducing or eliminating defects in products. This was not to be done by brute forced initiative, such as increased quality inspection, but by continuously improving the process from a system's standpoint. That is, products and processes had to be designed to be Six Sigma. The results of such design efforts had to be reduced variation, improved quality, increased productivity, and greater ease and efficiency in the operation of the process and the making of the product. This could only be done by characterizing, optimizing and controlling the total process, not just parts of it. It was equally important to reduce or eliminate errors and mistakes in all administrative, service and transactional processes in order to provide total customer satisfaction. So, Motorola applied the same concepts of quality to all aspects of their business.

By June of 1987 Motorola challenged its employees to start implementing Six Sigma in the administrative functions, "Sit down right now and start the analysis of your own department's activities, or your personal operating systems and procedures. Determine what you must do to achieve Six Sigma performance. You don't have to be a statistical expert to utilize the concept. All you have to do is be willing to modify your own modus operandi and your personal operating system, so as to eliminate defects and rejects in your personal work product."

On July 23, 1987, a memorandum was distributed to all the employees of Motorola Semiconductor Product Sector, welcoming all to the concept of Six Sigma performance. It also introduced a kit which was prepared to assist in understanding the concept of Six Sigma along with a videotape of Bob Galvin's message. It explained Six Sigma performance was a relationship between the performance and design level, or performance and tolerance levels. The concept was equally valid for manufacturing/design operations and support functions. The memorandum further clarified the concept was based upon zero-defects in production and administrative operations. It further explained Six Sigma performance objectives were being pursued across the Motorola Corporation and such objectives exceeded the performance yet achieved by most corporations. Finally, the memo emphasized to Motorola employees its conviction that only through Six Sigma could Motorola obtain the worldwide, best-in-class status in the community of industrial electronics corporations.

By March, 1988, Motorola came out with a course on "The Six Steps to Six Sigma". The course was more applicable to the administrative or service process and not to the improvement of technical processes.

However, "The Six Steps to Six Sigma" did make two things clear. First, the "Six Sigma Quality Program" was tied to Key Goals and Key Initiatives. The Key Goals were:

- Increase global market share
- Pursue best-in-class status in people, marketing, manufacturing, technology, product and service
- Superior financial results

The Key Initiatives were:

- Six Sigma quality
- Total cycle time reduction
- Product and manufacturing leadership
- Profit improvement
- Cooperation between organizations

Second, and perhaps most important, Motorola's definition of Six Sigma was radically different from the norm as understood by academia.

Motorola's Definition of Six Sigma

Motorola defined Six Sigma as having plus or minus six sigmas ($\pm 6\sigma$) or standard deviations within specification limits.

In other words, given a particular product characteristic which has a design specification, that design specification has an upper specification limit, USL, and a lower specification limit, LSL, these two limits demarcated a design tolerance. Motorola held the design tolerance should be such that it should allow to fit twelve (±6) sigmas or twice the process variation. The process variation had previously been defined as ±3 sigma, or six multiplied by the value of sigma. Motorola's approach was to take the particular product and measure the characteristic of interest and estimate its sigma, then the value of sigma should be such that twelve of them should fit within the specification limits. This was very different from what was understood or referred to as six sigma up to that time. Six sigma had always meant ±3 not ±6 sigma within specification.

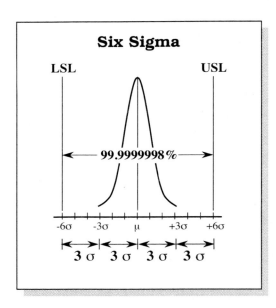

Motorola's new definition of the term Six Sigma - here

capitalized to make a distinction from the old six sigma - became plus or minus six, or twelve sigmas within specification limits.

Motorola had looked for a catchy name to shake up the organization when introducing the concept of variation reduction. In Six Sigma they found what they sought. But, had they possessed a more clear understanding of academia's terminology for six sigma, they might have named it Twelve Sigma or added the ± (plus or minus) to the term Six Sigma. As it turned out the term Six Sigma created a lot of confusion because of its conflict with academia's six sigma.

But, despite this, Six Sigma has become more than just a catchy name. It reflects a philosophy for pursuing perfection or excellence in everything an organization does. Six Sigma is probably the most successful program ever designed to produce change in an organization. It produced significant financial benefits to Motorola, but if we were to be cynical and strip the financial merits it produced, the Six Sigma program made about 100,000 people scattered all over the world, with very distinct responsibilities, educations, languages and cultures, be aware and focus on one single topic: reduce the value of SIGMA. And it did that instantly, like no other program ever. The synergy that Six Sigma created internally in the organization, and continuously creates in other organizations is overwhelming. The financial benefits it incurs are of course undeniable.

III. Embarking on Six Sigma

Why Embark on Six Sigma?

Six Sigma is a measure of quality and efficiency, but furthermore it is a measure of excellence. For an organization to embark on a Six Sigma program means delivering top quality service and product, while at the same time virtually eliminating all internal inefficiencies. It means having a common focus on excellence throughout the whole organization.

In manufacturing processes, embarking on a Six Sigma program means not just delivering defect-free product after final test or inspection - that can easily be accomplished while sustaining high levels of defective, rework, scrap and overall process inefficiencies. More importantly, it means delivering top quality product while concurrently maintaining in-process yields around 99.9999998%, defective rates below 0.002 parts-per-million and virtually eradicating defects, rework and scrap.

Also, other characteristics needed to sustain Six Sigma would be running processes under statistical control, controlling the input process variables (rather than the usual output product variables), maximizing equipment uptime and optimizing cycle time.

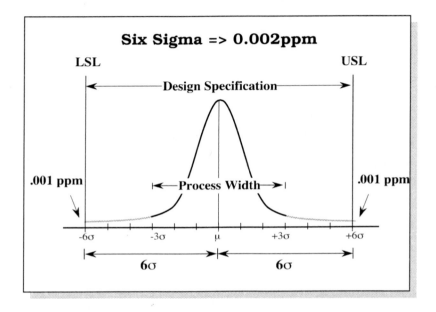

In administrative processes, this may mean not only the obvious reduction of cycle time in processes, but most importantly, eliminating the possibility for errors, mistakes and inefficiencies, as well as optimizing response time to inquiries, maximizing the speed and accuracy at which inventory parts and materials are supplied to requesters, and practically foolproofing these invisible processes against errors and inaccuracies.

What is the Goal of Six Sigma?

The ultimate goal of Six Sigma is to reduce defects, errors and mistakes to zero-defects and to reduce the sigma or standard deviation to a value that will allow twelve of them to fit between the specification limits. Concurrently, the average is kept as close as possible to the middle of the specification or nominal without allowing it to shift.

Why reduce variation, defects, errors and mistakes towards zero? Because it yields Customer Satisfaction, and happy customers keep on buying products or services. Happy customers usually tell their friends about how pleased they are with a product or service. But unhappy customers will usually tell everybody, even strangers, how displeased they are.

How Long does it take to Achieve Six Sigma?

Motorola in 1987 set a five year target to achieve Six Sigma. General Electric set itself a goal of becoming a Six Sigma quality company by the year 2000. This goal was established in 1996, when they initiated their full blown commitment to Six Sigma. Again, a five year target.

The initial training of on organization does not take but a few months. Within a few months teams are already working on characterization studies and improvement projects.

The full deployment of the Six Sigma program may take a few years. It is an intensive training and deployment process involving people from all levels of the organization. As they are trained and teams are formed, they are empowered - by the executive leaders - to apply tools and a methodology to characterize and optimize their processes. Every time a team completes an iteration of the methodology on a particular process, the process is improved to Six Sigma levels. The results are obtained at each iteration.

How long does it take for a company to achieve Six Sigma? It depends entirely on the number of people trained, the number of processes to be optimized, the number of iterations made and the level and degree of uniform, consistent and continuous conformance with the methodology. The more iterations of the methodology, the more processes are elevated to Six Sigma, the more process are at zero-defects, with no errors and mistakes. The rewards appear at every iteration.

Is Six Sigma ever Reached?

Of course Six Sigma is reached in every process, product or service to which the methodology is applied.

Would an organization be able to achieve a Six Sigma level of quality? It all depends on the level of commitment of the organization, the number of people trained and the number of iterations to be made.

Do you ever stop? Why would you want to stop? The

purpose of the Six Sigma program is to ingrain this methodology into everybody's work ethic and make it the company's culture.

Why is Six Sigma Needed?

Many successful companies have processes generating as much as 35,000 defects per million operations. Despite this, they are successful and they make a lot of profit. This level of performance is about 2.1 sigma. Now imagine, how much more profit they would be making if they were operating at a few defects per million operations, or operating at a Six Sigma level of almost zero defects. I recently worked with a company that produces engines. During the hands-on training, we applied the methodology to an engine boring process. The engine boring process was performing at a 1.57 sigma level, the number of defective cylinder heads was 164,795 per year with a total loss of $741,579. They were so accustomed to living with this condition and still being so successful, the company personnel felt the loss insignificant in comparison to the overwhelming amount of profit they made. But if you can save three quarters of a million dollars in less than three months by implementing Six Sigma, is it worth it? It is money in the bank.

Most companies do not even know at what level of defects they are operating, far less at what level of Sigma they perform. This information is not even available, nor have they even thought about it. Meanwhile these organizations are very inefficient and spend about 30% of their time fixing recurrent problems, correcting mistakes and fixing errors committed before. Some organizations live with their inefficiency and even factor it as part of doing business. A Six Sigma program eventually creates an organization intolerable of defects, scrap, rework, mistakes and errors. It creates an organization obsessed about making their processes robust against defects or errors, and about streamlining them so they are efficient and simple, operating with short cycle times and having no opportunities for mistakes.

What are the Benefits of Six Sigma?

First and foremost, the objective of any business is to make money. The undeniable objective of Six Sigma level performance is minimizing costs through reduction or elimination of non-value-added activity and maximizing quality output to realize optimum profit.

Implementing Six Sigma in an organization creates an internal culture of educated individuals in a standard methodology for characterizing, optimizing and controlling processes. Why processes? Because the repetitious activity involved in providing a service, or producing a product constitutes a process. Why optimize and improve the processes? So the processes are simplified, reducing the number of steps and making them faster and more efficient. At the same time these processes are optimized so they do not have a chance of producing defects and they present no opportunities for error or mistakes. Why go about eliminating defects, errors and mistakes? For two reasons. First, these make products and services more expensive. And the more expensive they are, the less likely people can or will buy them. Second, because defects, errors and mistakes upset customers, and dissatisfied customers either return products or do not buy services. As the number of customers upset with products or services increases, there is a tendency to lose market share. As market share is lost so is gross income. As gross income decreases, the organization can no longer hire or sustain employees. Without employees and income, the organization can no longer stay in business.

To What Processes is Six Sigma Applicable?

Six Sigma can be applied to every facet of a business, if the business facet is viewed as a system and treated as a process.

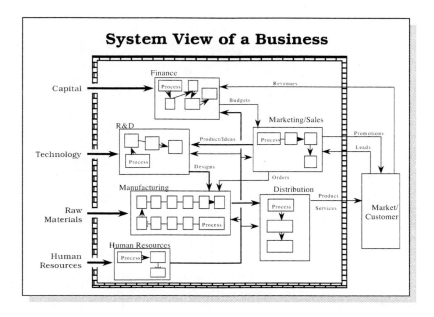

Six Sigma is applicable to technical as well as non-technical processes. A manufacturing process is viewed as a technical process. In it we have inputs, such as, piece parts, assemblies, sub-assemblies, products, parts, raw materials that physically flow through the process. Other inputs are temperatures, humidity, speeds, pressures, etcetera. There are a multitude of input variables that affect a process. A process also involves equipment, gauges, machines and tools - amongst other things - that produce the transformation of the input to an output. Finally, the output is usually a final product, a sub-assembly, an assembly, etc. In a technical process, the flow of the product is very visible and tangible. There are many opportunities for collecting data and measurements and in many instances variable data.

On the other hand, non-technical process are more difficult to visualize. Non-technical processes are administrative processes, service processes, transactional processes. In these processes the inputs may not be tangible, the outputs may not be tangible, and what is defined as the transformation may not be tangible. But, these are certainly processes and treating them as systems allows us to understand them better and eventually characterize them, optimize them, control them and, thus, eliminate the possibility for errors and mistakes. Generating a budget is an administrative process, selling a product over the phone is a service process, applying for a home loan is a transactional process.

Who Needs Six Sigma?

Let's analyze the conditions of two organizations, one doing badly, and one doing really well.

What could be happening in the organization doing badly?

The organization is experiencing poor quality in its products and is losing market share. It has, a product on the market but the competition has come up with one of its own and is gaining market share. How can Six Sigma help in this situation? Well, Six Sigma can be applied to the process of designing new products, making them more robust, and manufacturable with better quality and reliability and more fully reflecting customer needs in the process.

For the organization doing badly inefficiency and customer complaints have become commonplace. The inefficiency usually comes from performing process steps which are not necessary, take too much time, or involve so many individuals none of them see the consequences of their actions or the importance of their role in the process.

After all products are made by processes. So, if the organization and its people do not understand the science of their process, there is no way they can control, modify, optimize, much less, improve the process. It is not possible to improve something if it is not understood. It is necessary to first study it in order to know which variables affect and which do not affect the process.

The same is true for administrative, service and transactional processes. A process -whether technical or non-technical - delivers defects, errors or mistakes because it is not being done correctly. So, it has to be fixed or changed. To do this it must first be studied and understood.

Once known, the variables affecting the process can be manipulated in a controlled fashion to improve the process. And once it is known which variables truly influence the process, with a high level of confidence, it is possible to optimize by knowing what inputs to control to maintain the process at optimum output performance.

The M/PCpS Methodology delineates the process, streamlines the process by eliminating non-value added steps, and identifies the steps that are long, difficult and risky, and the steps where high incidence for mistakes are possible. It is through the M/PCpS Methodology that the organization will benefit by learning to become efficient and productive in their work process in order to achieve Six Sigma.

The M/PCpS Methodology teaches the steps to achieve Six Sigma. As a methodology, M/PCpS is itself a process that must be studied to be understood, and practiced repeatedly to be truly learned.

Let's now take a look at an organization doing very well. This organization increased its market share. It is a prosperous organization selling more products or services than before, needing more personnel, and greater capacity, to deliver more product or services in the same timeframe to meet the growing demand. Six Sigma is more important to the organization doing well than to the one doing badly. The organization doing well has more to loose than the one doing badly.

For the organization doing well the M/PCpS Methodology is the process to achieve Six Sigma and it is the methodology to remain at Six Sigma so the organization can also remain efficient, productive, cost effective and with good quality and especially, profitable. But most importantly, it is the way for the organization not just to thrive, but to truly develop and grow. Only by achieving and maintaining Six Sigma through the M/PCpS Methodology can an already successful organization go to the next level of performance. In the modern marketplace being competitive is not enough. The organization doing well must strive to excel through improvement and innovation to become the standard by which others benchmark themselves; to become "best-in-class" not just as products are concerned, but in service, administration and transactions as well. This is the next level of performance.

How do I know we need Six Sigma?

If customers are complaining about the quality or reliability of products, or about work or service quality, the organization probably needs to make a thorough assessment for the following signs:

- Loosing market share
- Taking high dollars

- Experiencing a heavy loss as a result of customer warranty returns and claims
- Invoices not paid on time due to customers complaints
- Wrong parts from suppliers
- Erroneous internal report information
- Unreliable forecasts
- Actuals frequently over budget
- Problems keep recurring and the same fixes have to be made repeatedly
- Designs for products extremely difficult to manufacture
- Scrap rates too high and uncontrollable
- Rework acceptable as normal production activity

What are the Major Differences between TQM and Six Sigma?

Although both TQM and Six Sigma are continuous improvement efforts, TQM is driven from the Quality department in a company and focuses on improving quality. Six Sigma is driven from the executive level of a company. Its focus is reducing variability (sigma) and eliminating defects, errors and mistakes and that will bring quality. Six Sigma focuses on the root cause - sigma and defects - and not quality itself, to achieve quality. Both TQM and Six Sigma focus on bringing satisfaction to the customer, both internal as well as external. TQM uses a number of tools to achieve total quality but does not specify the order in which the tools should be used.

Six Sigma on the other hand, uses a Methodology - M/PCpS - that presents the exact order in which the tools should be used and when not to use them. Six Sigma goes after characterizing the process regardless if it is a manufacturing process or a budgeting process.

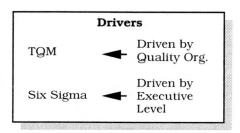

IV. Six Sigma Metrics and Statistics

Six Sigma Metrics and Associated Indices

Six Sigma uses metrics and indices to establish a baseline of where the organization is in relation to the goal of Six . Sigma. Why establish a baseline? If we are attempting to achieve a particular goal, we need first and foremost to know where we are. To know were we stand, we need to start taking measurements. Once we know where we are and where we want to go, we can now determine the gap that exists and at that point, we can assess the efforts and resources needed to reduce the gap, thus achieving our goal.

Motorola started their Six Sigma program by establishing a baseline to quantify their quality levels to January 1987 and then spread the achievement of Six Sigma over the next five years by establishing incremental goals. Then they tracked the improvement of their quality over the next five years, and developed a five year plan to achieve Six Sigma in everything they do.

The metrics and indices are extremely important. These indices also allow us to benchmark the organization, products, and services against competitors in the marketplace. It allows us to truthfully quantify if we are best-in-class or if the competition best-in-class.

Although I am here emphasizing the need for measurements, indices and metrics, do not loose perspective of what Six Sigma is all about. It is not about metrics. It is about improvements. The metrics are necessary, but they are the means not the end. Many organizations are just incorporating the metrics and they believe they are embarking on Six Sigma. Let me be blunt here! That is WRONG! The metrics alone do not bring the bottom-line improvements you are seeking.

Process Capability Indices

There are a few indices used in relation to the capability of a process. Capability is defined as the ability of a process to produce products within specification limits. The Cpk is the index of process capability. The Cp is the index of process potential. The Cpk and the Cp are mostly used in technical processes and seldom used in administrative, service or transactional processes. There are other indices quite useful in technical processes, such as the Cpm (off-center index) and the P/t ratio (process to tolerance ratio), but for all practical purposes, the Cp and the Cpk are sufficient.

Process Potential Index (Cp)

The process potential index, or Cp, measures a process's potential capability, which is defined as the ratio of the allowable spread over the actual spread. The allowable spread is the difference between the upper specification limit and the lower specification limit. The actual spread is determined from the process data collected and is calculated by multiplying six times the standard deviation, S. The standard deviation quantifies a process's variability. As the standard deviation increases in a process, the Cp decreases in value. As the standard deviation decreases (i.e., as the process becomes less variable), the Cp increases in value.

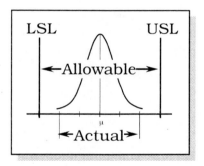

By convention, when a process has a Cp value less than 1.0, it is considered potentially incapable of meeting specification requirements. Conversely, when a process Cp is greater than or equal to 1.0, the process has the potential of being capable.

Ideally, the Cp should be as high as possible. The higher the Cp, the lower the variability with respect to the specification limits. In a process qualified as a Six Sigma process (i.e., one that allows plus or minus six standard deviations within the specifications limits), the Cp is greater than or equal to 2.0.

$$Cp = \frac{USL - LSL}{6 \cdot S}$$

However, a high Cp value doesn't guarantee a production process falls within specification limits because the Cp value doesn't imply the actual spread coincides with the allowable spread (i.e., the specification limits). This is why the Cp is called the process potential.

Process Capability Index (Cpk)

The process capability index, or Cpk, measures a process's ability to create product within specification limits. The Cpk represents the difference between the actual process average and the closest specification limit over the standard deviation, times three.

$$Cpk = \left\{ \text{Smaller of } \frac{\overline{X} - LSL}{3 \cdot S} \text{ or } \frac{USL - \overline{X}}{3 \cdot S} \right\}$$

By convention, when the Cpk is less than one, the process is referred to as incapable. When the Cpk is greater than or equal to one, the process is considered capable of producing a product within specification limits. In a Six Sigma process, the Cpk equals 2.0.

The Cpk is inversely proportional to the standard deviation, or variability of a process. The higher the Cpk, the narrower the process distribution as compared with the specification limits, and the more uniform the product. As the standard deviation increases, the Cpk index decreases. At the same time, the potential to create product outside the specification limits increases.

Cpk can only have positive values. It will equal zero when the actual process average matches or falls outside one of the specification limits. The Cpk index can never be greater than the Cp, only equal to it. This happens when the actual process average falls in the middle of the specification limits.

Parts-Per-Million (ppm)

The metric ppm or parts-per-million applies to defective product, or parts, as well as, to defects, errors and mistakes. So, in the language of Six Sigma we talk about defects-per-million, errors-per-million, mistakes-per-million, defectives-per-million and this last one is more known as parts-per-million defective.

All of these metrics are used to standardize the quantification of defectives, defects, errors and mistakes. Again, the common language and cultural change that Six Sigma brings into an organization. Why this standardization? So, we can communicate better and be able to equally compare our numbers as they may be coming from different parts of the organization.

The ppm estimates the number of units, piece-parts or products that are defective, should a million be produced. It could be a simple exercise of just taking a sample of products, inspect them and determine the number that are defective. Let's say in a sample of 30 products, 1 was defective. Then the fraction defective would be 1 divided by 30 and that is 0.033. If we make it a percentage, that is 3.3% not bad you might say. That equates to a ppm level of 33,333, this is very close to the process performance of most successful companies. In another case, we could have a fraction defective of 0.0009 or 0.09 percent. In many organization that is considered almost zero. But in Six Sigma terminology that is 900 ppm, still very far from the Six Sigma goal. So, the ppm metric gives better resolution

Sigma Level ($\pm$ xσ)	Cp	Cpk	PPM
[$\pm$ 1σ] ~ One Sigma	0.33	0.33	317,320
[$\pm$ 2σ] ~ Two Sigma	0.67	0.67	45,500
[$\pm$ 3σ] ~ Three Sigma	1.0	1.0	2,700
[$\pm$ 4σ] ~ Four Sigma	1.33	1.33	63.5
[$\pm$ 4.5σ] ~ Four and a half Sigma	1.50	1.50	6.9
[$\pm$ 5σ] ~ Five Sigma	1.67	1.67	0.6
[$\pm$ 6σ] ~ Six Sigma	2.0	2.0	0.002

[Assumptions: Normality, Stability and Distribution centered.]

for quantifying defectives, defects, errors and mistakes.

The ppm is a simple calculation, but that is when we determine it from inspection. In most cases, the response that we would be characterizing would be a characteristic as it deviates from its specification, and for that we use the Normal distribution.

What is the ppm for Six Sigma?

The parts-per-million defective associated with Six Sigma is 0.002 ppm. This value is about two parts-per-billion defective. The 0.002 parts-per-million is an estimate that stipulates, that if 1,000,000 units were produced, not even one would be defective. If one billion units were produced, only 2 would be defective.

Is Six Sigma 3.4 ppm?

Six Sigma is not 3.4 ppm. The whole misunderstanding about 3.4 ppm resulted from Motorola's document "Our Six Sigma Challenge". In it Motorola asserted if a process was made to be Six Sigma by having the design specifications be twice the process-width, the process would be extremely robust. Such a process would be robust, even if it was surprised by a significant or detrimental shift in average, as high as +1.5 sigma, the customers would not perceive a degradation in quality. At worst case, a shift of 1.5 sigma, would make a zero-defects product be 3.45 ppm and the customer would only perceive an increase from zero to 3 products defective, assuming a production run of 1,000,000. This was supposed to be the warranty Six Sigma processes brought to the customer, not actual ppm levels for Six Sigma. The problem became widespread, when Dr. Mikel Harry [1] attempted to find a mathematical justification for a ±1.5 sigma shift in average by erroneously quoting an article written by David H. Evans.

In the series of articles "Statistical Tolerancing: The State of the Art", and more specifically in Part III. Shifts and Drifts [4], Evans discusses a tolerance stacking problem in which multiple disks are staked to produce a final stack assembly. He states "...that a slight shift in the mean thickness of the disks could cause a drastic increase" in the fraction out-of-tolerance of the final stack assembly. He also states a good quality control program would detect any shift in means in the components or disks. But, he states a proposed solution suggested by A. Bender in setting tolerances, which is to take the variance of the linear combination of the individual disk variances, take its square root and multiply it by a factor of 1.5, and use this as the standard deviation of the final stack assembly.

In other words, Bender suggested amplifying the standard deviation by a factor of 1.5 to compensate for any shift in mean of any individual disk, and to compensate for the lack of prediction. Nowhere, do Evans or Bender suggest the mean be shifted by any constant, far less a 1.5 sigma shift. Furthermore, Evans states that "...it is almost impossible to predict quantitatively the changes in the distribution of a component [disks] value."

Dr. Mikel Harry had erroneously misinterpreted a 1.5 magnitude of inflating the estimator of the standard deviation with a shift in mean of 1.5 sigma.

What is a ±1.5 Sigma Shift?

The plus or minus 1.5 sigma shift surfaced when Motorola in their explanation of "Why Six Sigma?", used it as a worst case scenario of a significant shift in process average. They stated that a ±1.5 sigma shift would not show a detriment in the out-of-tolerance percentage to their customers if their processes were designed to have their specification limits be at twice the process width, or at Six Sigma levels.

It does NOT imply a process mean shifts about ±1.5 sigma over time or as an average.

Defective

A product or part is said to be defective when it does not conform to specification. A product could be defective or non-defective. A defective product may have one defect or many defects. A product to be defective may need only one defect. To have more defects does not increase the level of defective of a product. There are only two conditions in this classification, defective or non-defective, and this is referred to as a dichotomy. When we classify product by defective or non-defective we are in essence dealing with a binomial population and binomial distributions.

When our characteristic is of attribute type, that is, when the data collected is qualitative, then we make use of the binomial distribution. On the other hand, when our characteristic is of variable type, that is, when we can make quantitative measurements, then we use the Normal distribution, if that is the distribution the characteristic follows.

We know a characteristic is defective when its measurement is outside the specification limits. To measure the fraction defective, we use the areas under the normal distribution exceeding the USL (upper specification limit) and LSL (lower specification limit) and predict those areas using the tables for the Cumulative Normal Distribution or the Unilateral Normal Distribution, both in the Appendix.

Silicon Pressure Sensor Micromachining

To illustrate how to calculate the fraction defective and parts-per-million defective and the application of the Unilateral Normal Distribution, let's use an example of silicon pressure sensors. Silicon sensors are the eyes and ears of microprocessor based equipment used in biomedical applications. Silicon sensors such as disposable blood pressure transducers are used in the clinical care of patients undergoing post-cardiac operation intensive care. In many situations these silicon sensors operate in direct contact with the patient's body or fluids for long periods of time. These transducers continuously monitor the patient's blood pressure providing information about the patient's health and need for drug treatment.

In low pressure sensors, the silicon sensing diaphragm plays an important role and limits its performance. Thinner pressure sensitive diaphragms are used to for lower pressures. The pressure sensitivity, an important variable in pressure sensors, is related to the active diaphragm area and the diaphragm thickness. The in-process specification for diaphragm thickness is 8.0 ± 0.5mm. The performance capability of the silicon diaphragm micromachining is at (±) Four Sigma, and at a 64 ppm level.

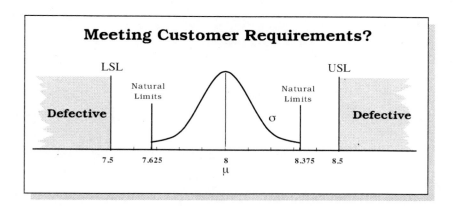

In a recent transfer of operations, the complete production line for the low pressure sensor products was moved to a new facility in the Asia-Pacific region. Upon arrival and setup of operations, various lots of production exhibited significant diaphragm thickness variability. Upon collecting data from various lots, the diaphragm thickness average is 8.35mm and the standard deviation is 0.25mm. It is apparent at the new facility the operation does not perform at the same level than prior to the move. It appears in the US operation, they had a more precise control of diaphragm thickness at the micron level. Now, we are interested in determining firstly, what is the current fraction defective and ppm level, and the new Sigma level of performance, and secondly the cost and profit impact.

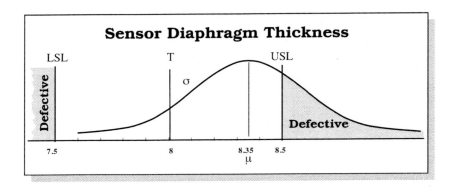

To compute the fraction defective, we first compute the z score for the upper specification limit, ZUSL, and then the z score for the lower specification limit, ZLSL. The ZUSL is calculated by taking the USL minus the average and dividing it by the standard deviation. This calculation, (8.5-8.35)/0.25 gives a value of ZUSL = 0.60, and we proceed to look for this Z score in the Unilateral Normal Distribution table in the Appendix. On the Z column of the table for the value of 0.60 we identify a whole row. This row has the fraction area under the curve that exceeds the Z scores starting with 0.60, and each consecutive entry (adjacent column) increments the Z score by a tenth (0.61, 0.62, 0.63, ...). For ZUSL of 0.60, the fraction area under the curve is 2.74E-01, or 0.274, this value is also referred to as the fraction defective exceeding the upper specification limit. If we multiply the fraction defective by 100, it will give us a percent defective of 27.4%, and if the fraction defective is multiplied by a million, this will result in the ppm level or parts-per-million defective of 274,000 ppm.

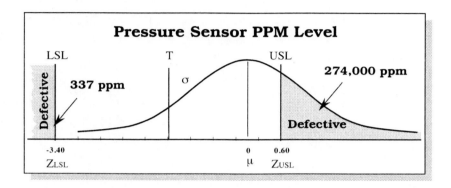

We proceed to do the same with the z score for the lower specification limit, ZLSL. The ZLSL is calculated in the same way, by taking the LSL minus the average and dividing it by the standard deviation. This gives a value of ZLSL= -3.40, and although the value is negative, we proceed to look for the positive value on the Unilateral Normal Distribution table, because the Normal distribution is bilaterally symmetrical. The table for the z score of 3.40 will give us the fraction area under the curve that is beyond the lower specification limit and considered a fraction defective. For ZLSL of 3.40, the fraction defective is 3.37E-04, or 0.000337, and by multiplying a million by the fraction defective we get a value of 337 ppm. Both these ppm levels are added together to obtain a total parts-per-million defective of 274,337 ppm.

The cost of processing low-pressure silicon sensors is $400 per 4-inch wafer. The output of a 4-inch wafer is up to

16,000 sensors per wafer. At the commodity price of 5 cents per sensor, the profit is at $400 per 4-inch wafer. At the current ppm level of performance of the Asia-Pacific fab, the yield per wafer would be reduced to an average of 11,610 die/wafer, bringing down the profit to about $180.50 per wafer. From this deterioration in ppm level, the projected loss in profit was annualize to be over 850,000 dollars.

Defects

A defect is a single instance of nonconformance with a particular requirement. A product or its piece-parts may have one or more defects. A single defect may qualify a product to be defective. A defective product may have one or more defects. The high incidence of defects in a production process is a nuisance that can significantly reduce the first-pass-yield, and increase the number of defective product, thus, creating scrap and rework. In any case, the presence of defects in production becomes costly and inefficient, and it is a burden to a production facility.

In order to eliminate the presence of defects, we must first find the variables influencing the occurrence of the defects (root cause), and then make the appropriate changes to reduce or eliminate the effect and then foolproof the process.

In the case of defective product, we use the proportion or the percentage of defective, and once that information is known, we can compute the percent of non-defective, because its total always equals 100%.

When dealing with defects, we seldom use the proportion or percentage, instead we deal in terms of incidence of the defect or with the count. So, collecting defects data is referred to as count data.

Consider, for example, a hardline cable TV service provider. These are the "Cable TV" companies. When we buy "pay-per-view", the networks transmit their signals to satellites in geostationary orbit above the Earth. These signals are then retransmitted from satellites to our local cable provider. The cable provider then amplifies and sends the signal through semirigid cable feeder lines. Along the feeder lines there are line taps that split the signal providing an output connection to the flexible coaxial cable into our homes and to our TV's. The

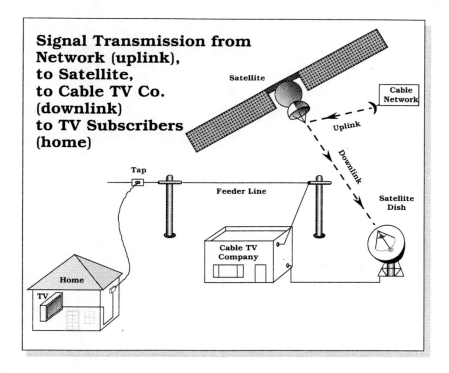

Signal Transmission from Network (uplink), to Satellite, to Cable TV Co. (downlink) to TV Subscribers (home)

Satellite

Cable Network

Uplink

Downlink

Tap

Feeder Line

Satellite Dish

Cable TV Company

Home

TV

transmission happens through a continuous passage of time in which a series of signals are sent. If the transmission service is perfect, then there is no interruption of the signal throughout this long series of transmission and the picture appears perfect on the TV screen. On the other hand, if on this continuum of time, the system experiences difficulties, then there would be defects in the transmission of the signals which would appear as breaks in the picture on our TV.

If these defects have a strong tendency of appearing at the start of service, then our impression of the service quality drops significantly. As the picture quality deteriorates then we start complaining to the service provider.

During a time interval, there are going to be millions of signals being transmitted. Now imagine the system has difficulty and a few defects are being transmitted in the stream of millions of signals. The defects are so few, it is virtually impossible to express them as a fraction, so we conveniently express them in terms of their incidence, or number of occurrences. Since these defects cannot be expressed in fraction form, we cannot use the binomial distribution to understand the behavior pattern of the process or system. The binomial distribution requires the percentage of defective signals so the percentage of non-defective signals can be computed. But, with defects, we can say in a time interval there are so many occurrences of defects transmitted in the signal, but what we cannot determine is how many non-occurrences of defects were present. And without this bit of information we lack the parameters for the binomial distribution.

In 1873 a French mathematician named Simeon Poisson figured out how to modify the binomial formula for cases when the fraction defective is extremely small, like in the case of isolated occurrences of defects. The modified formula then became the Poisson formula, and its distribution is referred to as the Poisson distribution. To apply the Poisson formula we need only determine the past (historical) average number of defects to predict quite accurately the probability of defects in the future and the distribution of defects. Some consequences of the Poisson distribution are the formulas for defects-per-unit and the first-pass-yield.

The purpose of utilizing defects is to quantify the goodness or badness of the process or system under study. Once we know how it performs and the incidence of defects, we can model it using the Poisson distribution and make predictions and inferences about the quality level in the future. With this knowledge, we could initiate process improvement and optimize it to Six Sigma performance levels. Then, we could monitor the process to make sure the defect level remains low and is no longer causing process deterioration.

Examples of situations in different work environments where the Poisson distribution could be applied are:
Banking .-
- Number of customers arriving for service at a teller in a new bank branch.
- Number of checks with no funds received by a bank per location per week.
- Number of home loan applications to non-qualifying customers per month.

Communications .-

- Number of dropped communications by the internet service provider per modem call from customers per day.
- Number of cellular phone connections dropped by the carrier per time frame.

Education .-

- Number of weapons brought by kids into the school facility during a particular time frame.
- Number of unexcused absences in a given school year.

Health Care .-

- Number of incorrectly prescribed medications.
- Number of lost or misplaced patient records.

Manufacturing .-

- Number of breakdowns per week of equipment in a production facility and its referral to maintenance.
- Number of defects in a spool of wire in a wire-bonding process for bonding microprocessors.
- Number of misplacement in surface mounted components in a printed circuit board per day.
- Number of empty cavities with no components in a reel of SM components for a chipshooter.

Transportation .-

- Number of shipments delivered to wrong

addresses per week.
- Number of pieces of luggage going to the wrong destinations in an airline per week.

Service .-
- Number of abandoned telephone calls from customers during a week.
- Number of telephone orders with wrong information per week, requiring sales call back.

Food Processing -
- Characterizing the number of raisins per box of cereals.
- Number of incorrectly processed orders at a fast food restaurant.

Errors or Mistakes

An error or mistake is failure to do what is correct. In administrative, service and transactional processes, there are a number of opportunities to make errors or mistakes. The errors and mistakes are also treated as isolated random occurrences in a continuum of time, and the proportion is not customarily used to quantify mistakes. Instead, the incidence of errors or mistakes is used and a count is produced. Similarly, as we did in counting defects, we do the same for errors and mistakes and make use of the Poisson distribution to understand the behavior pattern of the administrative, service or transactional process.

Defects-Per-Million Opportunities (DPMO)

The number of defects per million opportunities, or DPMO, is a metric for quantifying the total number of defects should a million be produced and dividing it by the total number of opportunities for defects.

In the DPMO formula, the numerator is the defects-per-million (dpm) level of performance of the process or operation and the denominator is a weighing factor representing the difficulty of the process or operation. This weighing factor - the total number of opportunities for defects - allows the DPMO to be used for comparing processes or operations with different levels of complexity against each other.

$$DPMO = \frac{dpm}{TOFD}$$

dpm = dpu x 1,000,000
TOFD = Total opportunities for defects

Imagine two production operations both producing defects and we want to compare them, but one is significantly more complex than the other.

In the simple one, an operator takes two parts, aligns them, and assembles them, producing a final assembly. This is a fairly easy, straight-forward operation.

In the other operation, the operator takes seven parts and

inserts them into a housing. The operator, then, takes four distinct sub-assemblies and puts them all together in the appropriate sequence onto the housing. The operator proceeds by taking eight identical screws and drives them into the sub-assemblies to secure them to the housing. Finally, the operator attaches a bar code label to the housing and a product label to the front of the housing.

This second operation is more complex than the previous one, and in essence, we assume it presents more opportunities for defects.

By computing the DPMO, we can compare the two operations by their incidence for defects weighted by their complexity. First we compute the total number of opportunities for defects. For the sake of simplicity let's assume the first operation has a total number of opportunities for defects equal to 2. On the second operation, we have identified 23 opportunities for defects:

Parts	Opportunities for Defects
Parts	7
Housing	1
Sub-assemblies	4
Sequence	1
Screws	8
Bar Code	1
Product Label	1
Total..........	23

This shows the second operation is a more complex

operation. Now we have the weighting factors for both operations, and we proceed to quantify the current performance of our two operations according to their incidence for defects. We collect data for a predetermined time and size of sample and compute the total number of defects found. Lets say the number of defects found were as follows:

Operation	Sample Size	Number of Defects
#1 (Simple)	2,500	95
#2 (Complex)	3,750	150

We then compute the defects-per-unit or dpu by taking the total number of defects found and dividing it by the sample size. After that, we compute the defects-per-million or dpm, by multiplying the dpu times 1,000,000, and finally the dpm is divided by the total number of defect opportunities to produce the DPMO.

Operation	dpm	DPMO
#1 (Simple)	38,000	19,000
#2 (Complex)	40,000	1,739

From these DPMO's we can determine the complex operation is performing much better in comparison to the simple operation. The DPMO applies a weight for the complexity of the operation to allow their comparison. On the other hand, if the presence of a defect makes the output of each operation a defective product then both of them are equally bad. Their First-Pass-Yield would be:

Operation	dpu	FPY
#1 (Simple)	0.038	96.27%
#2 (Complex)	0.040	96.08%

Great caution should be taken in using the DPMO in a technical process (manufacturing), because its interpretation may be misleading. The DPMO is a metric for the purpose of comparing the performances of different processes, products, facilities, equipment and operations given their complexity and inherent differences.

A Vice President of Operations might be interested in using a single metric to compare the incidence of defects in the Battery Assembly Operation for their Laptop Computers Division versus the Cellular Phone Assembly Operation of their Cellular Division. The DPMO can be computed for both operations once the number of opportunities for defects are identified.

Operation	Defects Opportunities	DPMO
Battery Assy Oper	384	215
Cellular Assy Oper	6,592	1,734

To further identify where within each of the assembly operations the majority of the defects are coming from, we could subdivide the Battery Assembly Operation into its major process steps and compute the DPMO by process step. The same thing could be done for the Cellular Phone Assembly Operation and breakdown the DPMO by each process step as shown below:

Process Step	DPMO
Screen Printing	114
Component Placement	1190
Glue Dispensing	45
Odd Components Manual Insertion	150
Reflow Soldering	35
Flex Soldering	10
Housing and Cover Assy	40
Final Testing	140
Label and Packaging	10
Total	**1734**

This could pinpoint the Component Inserter (Chipshooter) as the process step where the majority of the defects are coming from. This may suggest either preventive maintenance on the chipshooter itself, or a further investigation to identify the source or cause of defects such as to the component sequencer or part presentation to the chipshooter.

In some instances, the DPMO could further be converted into a sigma performance level. This is done using the PPM-versus-Sigma table in the Appendix and locating the DPMO value on the table, and associating it to a sigma level.

Operation	DPMO	Sigma Performance
Battery Assy Oper	215	3.70
Cellular Assy Oper	604	3.13

Errors-Per-Million Opportunities (EPMO)

The errors per million opportunities (EPMO) is a metric for measuring and comparing the performance of distinct administrative, service or transactional processes. The EPMO quantifies the total number of errors or mistakes produced by a process per million iterations of the process. It takes into account the opportunities for that process to have errors or mistakes. The premise is, if an administrative, service or transactional process is simple, it should not present too many chances for committing errors or making mistakes. On the other hand, if the process is complicated, cumbersome, difficult or not well defined, it may present many chances for errors and mistakes.

$$EPMO = \frac{epm}{TOFE}$$

epm = epu x 1,000,000
TOFE = Total opportunities for errors

To derive the EPMO, we first compute the errors-per-unit (epu). The epu is equal to the total number of errors found in a sample divided by the sample size. We then compute the errors-per-million (epm), by multiplying the epu times a million. Then, we divide the epm by the total number of opportunities for errors presented by the process.

The advantage of using the EPMO versus the epm is the EPMO takes into consideration the complexity of the process and the metric lends itself to comparing the performance of different administrative, service or transactional processes regarding their level of difficulty.

Assessing the Opportunities for Errors

The most important element in computing the EPMO is in assessing the total number of opportunities for errors in the process. To do that, first, break the process into smaller elements and carefully analyze them, so as to define the areas for errors and classify the different types of errors possible. Then allocate the errors to their position of origin using reference process steps designators and finally, compute the total number of errors by each process step and for the complete process.

Counting the Errors from the Process

Counting the total number of errors generated from the process is fairly simple. In administrative, service or transactional processes it is usually done by conducting an audit of the process and counting the total number of errors found. A large enough representative sample should be taken during. The number of errors found are then divided by the sample size to compute the epu and then converted into epm value.

The EPMO is then computed by taking the total number of errors found during the audit converted into errors-per-million and that value is divided by the total number of opportunities for errors.

Imagine we have two distinct administrative processes, and one is significantly more difficult than the other, and we would like to use a metric to compare them. One administrative process is the generation of invoices by the Billing department, and the other is the generation of payroll checks by the Payroll department. One administrative process is more complex than the other and their difficulty is correlated to a high incidence of errors. A simple process such as the generation of payroll checks may have about ten opportunities for errors. The process for generating invoices may have about thirty-five opportunities for errors. How can we compare these two distinct processes when one is more complex than the other, and has more opportunities for errors. The EPMO uses a weighting factor for opportunities for making errors or mistakes to account for the complexity of the process.

Let's assume in the payroll check process, it was determined there were 10 opportunities for errors. In the case of the generation of payroll checks by the Payroll department, the total number of opportunities for errors were computed as follows:

Parts	**Opportunities for Errors**
Work Hours	1
Overtime Hours	1
Futa	1
Suta	1
Withholding	1
SSN	1
Name	1
Address	1

Check Amount	1
Date	1
Total...............	**10**

An audit of the process was done over a period of one month, encompassing a sample of 1,400 checks. From the audit, 74 errors were found and the errors-per-million was computed as 52,857 epm. But, since this epm takes into consideration the process difficulty, we divide this number by the total number of opportunities for errors, and the EPMO is equal to 5,286.

We can further convert the EPMO into a sigma performance level. This is done by treating the EPMO as a ppm value and using the PPM-versus-Sigma table in the Appendix. We can then determine at what sigma level this administrative process is performing. From the table under an EPMO level of 5,286 we can approximate the sigma at 2,79.

Admin. Process	**EPMO**	**Sigma Performance**
Payroll Check Process	5,286	2.79 sigma
Invoicing Process	34,800	2.11 sigma

Statistical Assumptions

It should not be forgotten that Six Sigma, along with the Process Capability Index, Process Potential Index, and other subjects discussed here share certain basic assumptions. The two most important assumptions are:

- **Normality:** The response or characteristic's distribution follows or can be approximated by the Normal or Gaussian distribution.

• **Stability:** The pattern that results from plotting the data of the response or characteristic against time is under statistical control.

These assumptions should be tested prior to making predictions or inferences, especially in the application of Six Sigma to technical processes.

$$
\pm\ 6\sigma\ \textbf{implies}\quad
\begin{array}{l}
\text{Cp} = 2 \\
\text{Cpk} = 2 \\
\text{ppm} = 0.002 \\
\text{Normality} \\
\text{Stability}
\end{array}
$$

The Normal Distribution

The normal distribution, plays a significant role in Six Sigma, and is its underlying statistical model. The normal distribution is the most important continuous probability distribution in the field of statistics. It is also referred to as the Gaussian distribution in honor to Karl F. Gauss (1777-1855), who derived a mathematical equation for the normal distribution from a study of errors in repeated measurements of the same quantity. His work was published in 1809. However, the mathematical equation for the normal distribution was first derived by Abraham DeMoivre in 1733. The distribution was also known to Pierre Simon de Laplace no later than 1775.

Many engineering characteristics and physical phenomena can be approximated by the normal distribution. In many other instances when characteristics do not follow inherently the normal distribution but other distributions such as the Binomial or Poisson distribution, we can still use the normal distribution to estimate them.

The normal probability function relates the values of the characteristics with their probability of occurrence. Knowing that the sampling distribution follows the normal distribution allows the prediction of occurrence of events. This also allows the prediction of how many sigma away from the mean a particular observation falls.

$$y = \frac{1}{\sigma \sqrt{2\pi}} \, e^{-\frac{(x - \mu)^2}{2\sigma^2}}$$

The shape of the normal distribution is determined by its two parameters, the mean and the sigma, μ and σ respectively.

The **y** refers to the probability of occurrence or relative frequency of occurrence, and the **x** refers to the particular characteristic or response being measured. The total area under the curve produced by the normal function implies the probability of all values of the characteristic and its area are equal to 1.0.

So, the normal curve allows us to make predictions or estimates of probability between values in the x axis or response by computing areas under the curve between those particular values.

Let's use an example to illustrate the application of the normal distribution. Imagine we have a process that produces CPU microprocessors (such as the PowerPC or Pentium chips). We are interested in making predictions about the speed of the processors. The speed is measured in MHz (Megahertz). How would we proceed in our analysis? We might first take a representative sample of microprocessors, and predict its mean (μ) and sigma (σ), then do a goodness of fit test to find out if the sample frequency distribution (histogram) follows or can be approximated with the theoretical normal distribution. Once we prove we have a good fit, then we use the normal distribution to make predictions about the behavior of our real process. Assuming the microprocessors had a mean (μ) of 400 MHz and a sigma (σ) of 10 MHz, and a good fit with the normal distribution, we can take advantage of tables precalculated by statisticians to find areas under the curve for particular values.

So, between ±1 sigma away from the mean, lies about 68.26 percent of the area under the curve. With respect to our example, this implies that 68.26 percent of the microprocessors coming out of the factory, would have speeds between 390 MHz and 410 MHz. Between ±2 sigma of the mean, lies about 95.46 percent of the area and between ±3 sigma of the mean, lies about 99.73 percent.

Other percentage of areas under the curve of importance are:

Between	Area under the curve
±4σ	99.994%
±4.5σ	99.99931%
±5σ	99.999939%
±6σ	99.9999998%

The theoretical normal distribution has some characteristics that are of importance for Six Sigma. One of the most relevant ones is the areas under the curve for predicting probabilities.

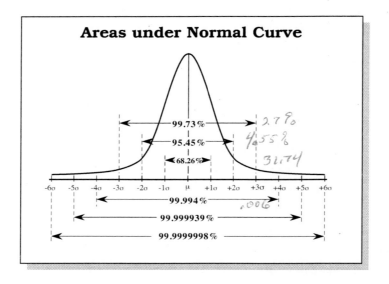

The normal distribution plays an important role in predicting fraction out-of-specification or parts-per-million (ppm) defective levels, as well as in analyzing process capability and in determining costs related to fraction-defective, rework and scrap.

Refer to the Cumulative Normal Distribution table in the Appendix for areas under the curve. The Appendix also has a Unilateral Normal Distribution table for areas under the tail of the distribution.

Justification for Six Sigma

The whole concept of Six Sigma has its roots in the application of statistics in engineering for the reduction of variability and quality control. It is due to this, that most consultants on Six Sigma are technically-oriented people and in most cases, engineers. Therefore, to understand the justification for Six Sigma we need to get a little bit technical.

Let's illustrate the rationale for pursuing Six Sigma in the technical arena. Usually a product has many characteristics. If we consider the simplest product, such as a match, we have at least 6 characteristics. In a more complex product, such as a hip replacement prosthesis, we may have as many as one hundred characteristics. On a more technically complex product such as a laptop computer, just the motherboard itself may have over two thousand characteristics, and that is excluding all the characteristics internal to the microprocessor, such as the Pentium Chip, which has over 5 million transistors. So, not even in the simplest of products do we find just a single characteristic.

However, for the time being, let us just consider one characteristic. If we have a product with a characteristic and the quality level or performance in producing this characteristic is such that its specification limits are equal to ±3 sigma. Then, we can infer that about 99.73% of the product would be good and about 0.27% would be defective by failing for that characteristic. The yield (the ratio of good units to bad as a percentage) of such a process would be 99.73%. This is referred to as a Three Sigma product (±3σ).

Historically, a process capable of producing 99.73% within specification was considered pretty good. In such a process, only 0.27 percent would be non-conforming to specification and rejectable. If we were to produce 1000 products, 997 would be good and only 3 would be defective. If we produced a million products, 997,300 would be good and only 2,700 would be bad and most likely reworked.

This does not seem to be too bad. But, since not even the simplest of products has only one characteristic, let's consider what happens when we have more than one characteristic. Let's imagine we have a process for assembling digital cellular phones and we have identified 239 characteristics. For the time being, lets imagine only two characteristics perform at a plus or minus three sigma level (±3σ). This implies each of the two characteristics have a fraction non-defective of 0.9973 and a fraction defective of 0.0027. If these characteristics are independent, then the yield would be 99.46% (0.9973 x 0.9973 = 0.9946).

This does not appear to be disconcerting, but if we had all the 239 characteristics performing at a Three Sigma (±3σ) level, each with a quality of 0.9973 fraction non-defective, then the yield for the digital cellular phones would be 52.40% i.e., Yield=100 x $(0.9973)^{239}$. So, for every one hundred phones started, only 52 would go through the entire production assembly line without a single defect, and about 48 of them would have at least one defect. If this company received an order for one million digital cellular phones, and 1,000,000 assemblies were started, then only 524,048 would be defect free, and the other 485,942 would have at least one defect per phone. It is obvious, to be competitive in the marketplace and to build product with zero-defects the first time around with no scrap, the quality at the characteristic level has to be much better than 99.73% or Three Sigma ($\pm 3\sigma$).

To be able to produce digital cellular phones with zero-defects, with no scrap, with no rework, the first time around, then you have to increase the performance capability at the characteristic level to Six Sigma, or 99.9999998 percent non-defective. If every characteristic in our digital cellular phones was performing at Six Sigma, then the First Pass Yield would be 99.99995% (100 x $\{0.999999998\}^{239}$).

In our particular example of digital cellular phones, if all 239 characteristics are Six Sigma, and we produced one thousand digital cellular phones, all would be defect-free. Furthermore, if we produced 1,000,000 digital cellular phones only one might have defects or be defective, and the other 999,999 would be defect-free. In this case, there would be no need to have a rework line, cost of rework personnel and equipment, would be saved and additional savings in product cycle time and predictability on on-time delivery would be realized. Also, since the First Pass Yield is so high, this production line would have minimum to no scrap. Making all characteristics Six Sigma, makes the process be defect free, cost-effective, and potentially, very profitable.

V. Strategy for Implementing Six Sigma

How to Embark on Six Sigma?

In essence, Six Sigma means overall excellence, not only in the finished product, but in the administrative, service and manufacturing processes throughout the organization. However, when embarking on a Six Sigma program, the typical organization simply explains what Six Sigma is and tells everyone in the organization to just to it. This approach is clearly not enough for such a demanding level of excellence.

The problem this leaves is numerous questions unanswered, directions undefined and everybody - in particular, the inexperienced - scrambling to invent their own version of what a Six Sigma program is or ought to be, and how it should be carried out. So, it becomes a free-for-all that yields all too few successes, lowers the acceptance of the program and its expectations, and assures a shortened life-cycle for the program.

What is needed, then, is a practical strategy encompassing all the necessary elements for a successful Six Sigma quality program.

Strategy for Implementing a Six Sigma Program

Over the last decade, much has been written about Six Sigma Quality, but even today, very little is truly understood about how it should be implemented. Nobody has ventured to propose a standard, holistic approach to implement it.

What follows is a road map for the implementation of such a program. It is based on the approach I developed for characterizing, optimizing and controlling a process to Six Sigma levels and supported by years of hands-on implementation experience, including seven years implementing Motorola's corporate Six Sigma Quality Program.

Six Sigma Challenge

Once the executive leaders of the organization have concurred to implement the Six Sigma Program, they have to impart the challenge to every individual in their organization.

The Six Sigma Challenge involves everybody in the organization, not only the people close to production - for whom it is very easy and obvious to implement a program that includes indices and measurements because the process is physical and tangible - but also the administrative and service providers within the organization.

Every individual in the organization provides a service. In a Six Sigma company the individuals assess their job function or role with respect to how it improves the organization. They define what would be the ideal of excellence (goal) in their service; after which they quantify where they are currently (status quo) with respect to this ideal; and then they work to minimize the gap in order to achieve Six Sigma by the goal's due date.

Six Sigma Executive Directive

The executive leaders of the organization express their commitment to converting the company to a Six Sigma organization by issuing an Executive Directive. The Executive Directive establishes the Challenge, the Vision, the Customer Satisfaction Promise, the Goal, the new Indices of measurement and the new way of operating the company. It draws the line between the old ways of doing business and the new way of working towards excellence and establishes a common goal for everybody in the organization: reduce variability (sigma) in everything they do. The Executive Directive calls for employee orientation, training and indoctrination of every individual through, at a minimum, an 8-hour course in "Achieving Six Sigma".

Role for Everybody

Six Sigma involves everybody in the organization. Every individual plays a significant role towards bringing the company to a world-class performance level. At the management level, managers are selected as champions or Team Mentors, their responsibility being to charter teams to engage in specific projects of improvement or characterization studies. Individuals with ability to grasp technical matters and with a strong know-how in their specific business are selected to be Team Leaders. These Team Leaders are responsible for the teams and lead them towards optimizing the processes under improvement towards Six Sigma. On each team formed, particular individuals that have talents and experience in the project's subject or process knowledge are chosen to be Team Members. The Team Mentors, Team Leaders and the Team Members are the ones that do the transformation of the organization from the ground level up.

Standardization

To successfully reach Six Sigma, the program must have a standard methodology. What the organization and all its employees must do to reach Six Sigma has to be very well defined and has to be standardized throughout the whole organization: There are 1000 ways to get to Rome, but the most efficient way is a straight line.

If the methodology for attaining Six Sigma is left undefined, there will be individuals in the organization who will try to invent and find their own way. It will not take too many of such individuals to de-rail the implementation of the program.

Standardizing the methodology to achieve Six Sigma, allows all individuals within the organization to focus on their individual projects on reducing the standard deviation, rather than being preoccupied and confused about what to do or how to do it.

The standardization of statistical methods and the methodology to achieve Six Sigma creates a common language and a common cause for everybody.

Many organizations implementing other non-standardized programs get stuck in arguments and disagreements over the methods and they never move forward. Eventually such non-productive activities tire everybody down and interest and enthusiasm for the new program quickly wanes and dies.

Road Map for Achieving Six Sigma in Technical Processes: Manufacturing and Production Processes

A methodology to achieve Six Sigma for technical processes, such as manufacturing and production processes, should be used throughout the whole organization. The standardization of the use of statistical methods establishes a common approach that speeds up the execution of Six Sigma characterization studies. It also creates a common language by which the individuals can communicate and compare results. The technical process methodology to achieve Six Sigma is the

M/PCpS Methodology. It is a step-by-step systematic approach to achieve improvements in technical processes and is designed exclusively to support Six Sigma efforts.

Road Map for Achieving Six Sigma in Non-technical Processes: Administrative, Service and Transactional Processes

Non-technical processes, such as purchasing or finance department functions, are considered invisible processes because their elements are not physical or tangible like the elements of production processes. Non-technical processes, due to their intangibility, are not as easy to define, quantify, optimize and control to Six Sigma levels.

Nevertheless, a methodology for characterizing and optimizing non-technical processes, such as administrative, service and transactional processes, to Six Sigma levels should also be equally standardized throughout the whole organization. In most cases, in non-technical processes, these studies are referred to as improvement "projects" because not all characteristics are optimized as in technical processes; usually, only a few critical-to-quality characteristics are optimized to Six Sigma levels in non-technical processes.

The methodology to achieve and sustain Six Sigma in non-technical processes has been carefully designed into the M/PCpS Methodology for administrative, service and transactional processes. It is also a step-by-step approach divided into five stages to achieve Six Sigma performance levels improvements. The sequence of this methodology is significantly different from the application to technical processes. The tools, methods and techniques change because the statistics are mostly non-parametric.

Quality Goal

An important aspect of the Six Sigma program is total process characterization, which involves optimizing all manufacturing processes to a very high Cp and Cpk value of 2. It is the achievement of this value that marks the success of a team in reaching Six Sigma. It is imperative that a goal of 2 in Cp and Cpk be established by the organization. This goal should be tied to the Quality goal of the organization. If the organization does not have an official goal, one should be established and announced throughout the whole organization by means of an executive directive.

The Six Sigma goal is to get as close as possible to zero-defects. Therefore, the Quality Goal should not be zero-defects; zero-defects is by default an impossibility and simply unreasonable. The Quality Goal should be a value, such as .002 parts-per-million defective or ± 6 sigmas within specification limits or some other challenging but achievable value that is quantifiable. A Six Sigma Quality goal sets the requirements of the Cp and Cpk to be equal to 2.0. This value is reasonable as well as achievable and would bring considerable profits to the organization.

Deployment Plan

To be able to keep the Six Sigma program focused, scheduled and running on time a Deployment Plan has to be designed and established. Teams and their members have to be identified, and the process studies and improvement projects have to be scheduled. Critical processes should be scheduled first and the Deployment Plan should be reviewed on a quarterly basis.

It usually takes a team working a few hours a week, for a few months, to perform a characterization study or an improvement project on a process. The total characterization and optimization of processes in a site may take continuous efforts over a few years. During that period of time, it is necessary to make an investment of resources, time and money.

Process Classification

To establish an order in which the process steps or operations are scheduled for process characterization studies or improvement projects, the process steps should be classified according to critical impact on the final characteristics critical-to-quality. To do this:

1. Form a team of individuals with macro and micro knowledge of the process or operation.
2. Identify all the process steps for a particular product line or business operation.
3. Go through each process step, starting with the first

process step.

4. Identify all the response variables for each process step.

5. Classify each process step as critical (c), major (M), or minor (m) with respect to how it impacts the final critical-to-quality characteristics.

Once all the process steps are classified, schedule them into the Deployment Plan; scheduling the critical first, then the major, and finally the minor process steps.

Monthly Review

The Six Sigma program requires a review, as well as an audit, to make sure everything is progressing correctly as planned.

On a monthly basis, teams are invited to present the progress of their process characterization studies and process improvement projects. This review meeting should be open to anybody who wishes to attend. Members of all teams, as well as management, should be invited to attend.

Presenting teams should show their progress, road-blocks, milestones, needs and findings. Guidance and support should be given by management and team mentors so teams may resume or continue their progress.   ·

Team Presentations

Studies and projects defined in the Deployment Plan are assigned to teams for improvement and achievement of Six Sigma. The teams apply the standardized methodologies to achieve Six Sigma and present their progress.

Presentations by the teams are done using standard formats for quick, direct and efficient performance. The emphasis of the presentation is data, documentation, and significant improvements. Presentation of the raw data is as important as team conclusions drawn from the data. As the projects progress, documentation is also generated and archived with the process owners, and the knowledge acquired by the team is preserved for posterity. A Six Sigma process improvement book is kept in the production or business operation area for documenting all efforts related to the process.

External and internal company experts are invited to attend these team presentations. The knowledge acquired by the team is shared with the attendees during the presentations and the two-way dialog creates a synergy for learning, sharing and experimenting. Management participates in these presentations by providing support, commitment and keeping the team in focus with the objectives of the organization.

Documentation

At every stage of the standard methodology to achieve Six Sigma, there should be a well-defined expectation and documentation requirement for the studies or projects. Documentation should be mandatory at each presentation and should be previewed by team mentors. The documentation is necessary for preserving the knowledge gathered and what has been learned about each particular process.

This documentation is then archived for future use by other teams as they study similar processes. It may also serve to fulfill the documentation requirements of ISO-9000, QS-9000 and FDA's Good Manufacturing Practices.

Bimonthly Progress Tracking Report

The site coordinator of the Six Sigma efforts should request bimonthly reports from each team leader to track and report the progress to the executive management. This bimonthly reporting avoids any surprises of non-progress from teams during the Monthly Reviews. The site coordinator then submits a bimonthly progress report to management summarizing all team activities. Progress towards the achievement of Six Sigma is compared to the Deployment Plan goals, and actual versus scheduled times are measured and tracked to keep the whole Six Sigma program in focus and in motion.

Award Recognition

To recognize and promote the interest of the teams, an award should be given to each member of the team that successfully completes the full characterization of a process and achieves Six Sigma. The award comprises three things: an award plaque, an attachment, a pin and enrollment in the Six Sigma Competition. The award plaque should be designed so attachments for each Six Sigma study or project completed by the individual participant can be attached for subsequent nominations.

Six Sigma Competition

Once a year, all studies and projects achieving Six Sigma levels of improvement participate in the Six Sigma Competition. Teams present their studies and projects, their approach and their improvements. A group of expert judges assess the teams' roles and improvements to ensure they meet evaluation criteria and, by a process of elimination, a winner is selected.

In this event, members of the organization get to see and experience what the organization is striving for in terms of quality, commitment, improvement, efficiency. Thus, they experience a reaffirmation of the organization's commitment to achieving Six Sigma. It also allows the organization to show how much it values the individual and team contributions and achievements. The Six Sigma Competition is empowerment by show and action.

How Much does Six Sigma Cost?

Many organization are interested in knowing how much

it costs to achieve Six Sigma. That depends on a couple of factors: on the organization's current performance level in comparison to Six Sigma goals and on the level of commitment in achieving those goals.

For example, a Japanese client that I visited a year ago, who has captured a market niche through excellence in design, research and outgoing product quality, had an interest in Six Sigma. If this market leader delivers an excellent outgoing quality in their product, but maintains a significant internal in-process scrap level, then this organization's "performance level of excellence" is still far from Six Sigma. Therefore, this market leader would need a strong level of commitment to bring their internal level of performance to Six Sigma.

In 1997, Jack Welch's commitment to Six Sigma efforts at GE amounted to a $300 million expenditure to enjoy a $600 million benefit.

What are Green Belts, Black Belts, Master Black Belts and Champions?

The Black Belt program was started by Motorola's Six Sigma Research Institute (SSRI) in 1991. The SSRI was a small branch of Motorola University, whose mission was to pioneer new tools, methods and approaches in the quest for Six Sigma. By 1994 the Institute fell short of its promises and was disbanded.

The "Black Belt program" includes the following hierarchy:

- Champions
- Master Black Belts
- Black Belts
- Green Belts

Although the Black Belt labels are a clever way of branding the roles of individuals supporting and making the changes in an organization, it undoubtedly brings a lot of confusion as the roles are vague and not cast in stone. To aid the understanding of the Black Belt labels, the following describes their roles.

Champions or Team Mentors

Team mentors are managers at different levels of the organization who define the studies or projects. A typical study or project is initiated after assessing its potential to realize savings in the neighborhood of $75,000 annually. The team mentor is not an active team member nor does he or she have an active role in the team's activities. Their function is to be informed and keep track of the team's progress and, to provide high management visibility, commitment and support to empower team members for success. Team mentors provide strategic direction for the studies and projects and ensure that changes, improvements or solutions are implemented. They officially announce the team's study or project completion after all objectives are met and documentation completed. Finally, they request presentations to upper management.

Master Black Belts or Site Coordinators

Site Coordinators are responsible to coordinate the Six Sigma program at the site level. They are full-time positions, one hundred percent dedicated to support the teams and the Team Leaders or Black Belts. They act as experts resources to all their teams and provide coaching, just-in-time training and statistical expertise. They are the ones that work with the Team Mentors to address roadblocks that impede a team's success. The Site Coordinators organize the monthly study and project reviews and assist teams in their presentations. Together with the Team Mentors, they determine team charter, goals, and members. They also formalize the studies and projects, and provide management leadership with progress reports.

Black Belts or Team Leaders

Although one hundred percent dedicated to support their teams, Team Leaders do not need to be full-time positions. They are responsible for implementing the methodology that will achieve Six Sigma in their studies or projects. They are active members of the team and are in charge of overall coordination of team activities and progress; assigning responsibilities to all team members, tracking the team's goals and plans, and managing the team's schedules and administrative duties. Finally, they are accountable to the Team Mentors for bottom-line improvements in the studies or projects, and for achieving annually-projected Six Sigma goals. The improvements have to demonstrate substantial dollar savings and significant difference in reducing variation, defects, errors and mistakes.

A current trend occurring in the business market-place is that Black Belts are high demand and are being hired away as fast as organizations are training them.

Team Leaders are also referred to as Process Improvement or Variation Reduction Leader.

Green Belts or Team Members

Team Members are the employees who maintain their regular jobs but are assigned to one or more teams given their know-how or background on the selected studies and projects. They have full responsibility as a team member in the project but they do not devote all their time to the project as does a Team Leader. They are expected to accept willingly and carry out all the assignments between the meetings, devote time and effort towards the success of the team, do research when there is lack of knowledge, and investigate other alternatives when necessary.

Is New Personnel needed for Six Sigma?

New personnel is not particularly needed for achieving Six Sigma. An objective of Six Sigma is to bring about a cultural change in the organization, and to prepare employees to use a methodology proven successful in other companies. Such preparation does not consist of just training four people, but the entire organization, making them realize they have the power for improving quality. It is not about delegating quality away to just a few current employees or even to a few, newly hired, presumed experts. It is about teaching new methods, techniques, tools and metrics and about demonstrating how to use them to everyone so everyone can understand the relevance of the methodology to the work they do.

Are Full-time Employees needed for Six Sigma?

Full-time Site Coordinators may be needed, depending on the size of the organization. And, depending on the number of studies and projects, full-time Team Leaders may be necessary as well. A Site Coordinator may supervise about ten Team Leaders, and a Team Leader may facilitate and manage successfully two teams.

A full-time position dedicated to bring about the Six Sigma cultural change in the organization and be involved in the studies and projects would definitively increase the success and financial rewards of the program.

How to Overcome Resistance and Achieve Buy-in?

To overcome resistance and achieve buy-in, the change needs to be initiated at the top of the organization. The most crucial change in an organization to implement Six Sigma successfully is that the Management Leadership - the CEOs and their staff - be convinced and demand Six Sigma be the way for running their business.

As the top Executive Leadership leads the Six Sigma cultural change, the rest of management will follow, and it will trickle down to the employees involved in the administrative, service and manufacturing processes.

This is the ultimate lesson learned from implementing Six Sigma and, for that matter, any revolutionary change in an organization. CEOs must be the ultimate leaders in the Six Sigma program: Jack Welch does it for GE, Larry Bossidy does it for Allied Signal, and Bob Galvin did it in 1987 for Motorola.

Tools Used to Achieve Six Sigma

There are a number and variety of tools, techniques and methods used in the quest for Six Sigma, and there are significant differences in their application to Technical and Non-technical processes. Here are a few:

Action Planning	Affinity Diagrams
Analysis of Variance	Bar Charts
Benchmarking	Binomial Distribution
Box Plots	Box-Behnken Designs
Brainstorming Sessions	Brainwriting
C&E Matrix	Corrective Action Logs
Cause & Effect Diagrams	Central Composite Designs
Change Acceleration Process	
Check Sheets	Chi-square Testing
Concentration Diagrams	Concordance Analysis
Control Charts	Cost/Benefits Analysis
Cumulative Count Charts	Cycle Time Analysis

Decomposable Mapping

Defects per Million Opportunities

Defects-per-milion   Defects-per-units

Descriptive Sensory Analysis

Descriptive Statistics   Destructive Gauge Analysis

Errors per Million Opportunities

Errors-per-million   Errors-per-units

EVOP   Facilitation

Flowcharting   FMEA's

Fractional Factorial Designs

Full Factorial Designs   Hierarchical Designs

Histograms   Hypothesis Testing

Likert Scales   Macro & Micro View

Manual-Process Performance Width Plots

Meetings Management

Multiple Regression Analysis

Non-parametric Statistics   Normal Distributions

OCAP's

Orthogonal Arrays   Parametric Statistics

Pareto Diagrams   Pie Charts

Plackett-Burman Designs   Poisson Distribution

Positrol Plans & Positrol Logs

Possibility Analysis   Procedure Sheets

Process Capability Analysis Process Mapping

Process Potential Analysis   Project Management

ProSolution Matrix   Repeatability Analysis

Reproducibility Analysis   Root Cause Analysis

RSM   Run Charts

Sampling Plans   Scatter Diagrams

Scoring & Ranking   Sigmas

Split Plot Designs   Storyboarding

Stratification Analysis
Tolerancing
Variation
Workstandards

Team Chartering
Value Analysis
Voice of the Customer

Which particular tools, techniques and methods and the order in which they should be applied, is determined and defined by the M/PCpS Methodology.

VI. The M/PCpS Methodology to Achieve Six Sigma

What is a Methodology?

A methodology is more than just a method - an orderly, logical or systematic way of accomplishing something. It is a logically, systematically and clearly organized set of tools, techniques, methods, principles and rules for use as a guide and a step-by-step approach to achieve something - something like the study, analysis or evaluation of a particular subject.

A sound methodology will provide a proven approach, a step-by-step procedure that can be easily followed by all. This means selecting the right methods, tools and techniques - and the proper formulations, when necessary - and, then, setting them in the right sequence and, finally, establishing the right set of rules and procedures.

The M/PCpS Methodology for the achievement of Six

Sigma is a logically, systematically and clearly defined and arranged set of statistical, mathematical, business and behavioral tools, techniques, principles and rules used sequentially, in a step-by-step manner, to characterize, optimize and control a process. In addition, the M/PCpS Methodology contains built-in milestones and documentation requirements to ensure everything is on-track and built-in safeguards to avoid going off-track.

Why Standardization of a Methodology?

On a team newly formed to characterize or optimize a process, each member usually has in mind a personal methodology, or sequence of steps, for achieving the task. The personal methodologies of each individual are based on their own past experience and involvement in earlier problem-solving projects.

Each team member will attempt to convince the team to follow their set of steps. This often creates arguments, wastes time in nonproductive meetings, and creates an atmosphere of confusion, disorder and lack of clear direction. Sometimes, the team members may lose interest and fail to cooperate because of their disagreement with the prevailing methodology.

To avoid these inefficiencies, two ingredients are necessary: Standardization and a sound methodology. The Machine/Process Characterization Study, M/PCpS, is a proven approach which provides the steps to follow in characterizing and optimizing technical and non-technical processes, thus, eliminating lost time and money in studies or projects that will not yield results.

Standardization eliminates the necessity for a team to design a new methodology for every study. The M/PCpS Methodology frees up the team to concentrate on the particular process - its variables, characteristics and behavior, and its analysis and improvements - rather than having to concentrate on developing a methodology. Standardization creates a common language when communicating about characterizing processes and provides the team a common direction. Managing and tracking the progress of the studies and projects is simplified, because each stage of the M/PCpS Methodology has a clear and predictable outcome.

Achieving Six Sigma performance levels is not an easy matter and often requires significant company time, efforts and funding. But most importantly, it requires a sophisticated improvement methodology composed of sound statistical tools arranged in a logical and systematic order of progression.

M/PCpS is an integration of a multitude of techniques: Team & Project Management, Benchmarking, Structured Problem Solving, Measurement System Analysis, Process Capability Analysis, Design of Experiments, and Statistical Process Control, to name a few. The M/PCpS Methodology has been tailored to two fundamental types of processes. Technical processes, such as manufacturing processes, and non-technical processes, such as administrative, service or transactional processes. Why is that? The reason is experience has demonstrated the techniques, methods, tools and most importantly, the statistical methods, are different than the ones utilized in technical process. In non-technical processes the characteristics follow non-normal distributions in general.

The M/PCpS Methodology for Technical Processes: Manufacturing and Production Processes

The M/PCpS Methodology is a step-wise analytical investigation using a standardized approach for determining the current capability of a process and for identifying and reducing or eliminating its major sources of variability. A study does not end until the goal capability (Cpk=2.0 or Six Sigma) is achieved or further investigation is no longer economically feasible. The methodology is divided into five progressive stages:

Stage 1:   Process Delineation
Stage 2:   Metrology Characterization
Stage 3:   Capability Determination
Stage 4:   Optimization
Stage 5:   Control

The Machine/Process Characterization Study defines a standard methodology for the purpose of characterizing and optimizing equipment and manufacturing processes. The five stages present a logical progression and a sequence of events designed in such a particular order to preserve and guarantee mathematical and statistical assumptions throughout the analysis. The standard forms and worksheets of the M/PCpS Methodology lead the practitioner through all important steps necessary to achieve capable manufacturing processes. They also become part of the documentation of the studies which are then stored in a computer database system for sharing with other manufacturing sites.

1st Stage: Process Delineation

The purpose of this stage is to thoroughly describe the machine and process under study. This is done by dissecting the machine and process into its functional characteristics and then continuing by identifying all the independent variables in each functional characteristic. Once this is done, all the response variables or dependent variables are listed and ranked according to their interrelationship with the independent variables into the C&E Cross-reference Table. The C&E Cross-reference Table is very critical and is used throughout the study, and is the key for successful statistical experimentation.

2nd Stage: Metrology Characterization

The second stage defines the metrology needed to evaluate the response variables under investigation and quantifies the amount of variation it brings into the overall study. This stage defines and identifies the necessary techniques to apply to quantify this variability, whether the measurement system is destructive or non-destructive.

3rd Stage: Capability Determination

The objective of this stage is to determine the current capability of the machine and/or process by running product through the process at known optimum levels. It is in this stage data is collected for the purpose of making predictions and inferences about the behavior of the process through time. Descriptive statistics are computed to understand the central tendency and variability of the process.

Goodness-of-fit tests are done to validate the shape of the distributions. Then the data is analyzed for stability and statistical control, and studies of repeatability, potential and capability are conducted. By going through these levels of detail, the individuals conducting and participating in the study gain exceptional knowledge of the process that lead them to conducting very productive statistical experimentation and optimization.

4th Stage: Optimization

Optimization is the most important stage because it focuses on reducing the amount of variation found in the previous stage. Reduction of variability (standard deviation or sigma) is the solution to many manufacturing problems, especially when processes are found not to be capable, Cpk is less than 1.0, or when they have a capability less than the goal of a Cpk of 2.0.

Statistically designed experimentation is the primary

tool used in the optimization stage. First, theories are formulated and then converted into statistical problems (hypothesis), and then proven or disproven with statistical tests. These tests are of various types: parametric tests, non-parametric tests, single factor, and multi-factor experiments. During optimization, statistically designed experiments are conducted with the following objectives in mind: a) to center the distribution of the response variables against the specification limits, b) to reduce the amount of variation (standard deviation) in the response variables, c) to determine the main and interactive effects of the "vital few" independent variables, and d) to identify the optimum levels of those independent variables.

The different experimental designs frequently used in this stage are: Full Factorial, Fractional Factorial, Orthogonal Arrays (Taguchi designs), Plackett-Burman screening designs, and Central Composite designs to name a few. Some techniques for optimization are: Response Surface Methodology (RSM), Evolutionary Operations (EVOP), or Regression Analysis.

5th Stage: Control

The fifth and final stage in the M/PCpS Methodology is the Control stage. After the process has been made capable and stable through Optimization, necessary preventive and proactive controls are set in place. Control charts are the last tools to be implemented when analyzing manufacturing processes or conducting process capability studies. Unfortunately, because control charts are simple in nature, they are usually the first tools to get implemented. This often leads to frustration on the part of operators and engineers when confronted with out-of-control conditions for which the corresponding influential independent variables are not known. For this reason, process controls, such as control charts and positrol plans, are not implemented until a complete understanding and characterization of the machine and process (main and interactive effects of the "vital few" independent variables) is achieved. It is at this stage when the knowledge obtained from the previous four stages is transferred to production and to the operators.

At this final stage, critical response variables are monitored and controlled with control charts techniques. The important independent variables are monitored with a positrol plan and positrol log. These will assure the independent variables will remain at their optimum levels as they were defined in the Optimization stage. The "vital few" independent variables which influence variability and whose optimum levels are difficult to control and maintain in a stable condition (even after optimization) are monitored with the positrol plan and with control charts. At this point, the whole sub-process and machine are locked at the optimum levels and the response variables should exhibit minimal variation.

The M/PCpS Methodology for Non-Technical Processes: Administrative, Service and Transactional Processes

For non-technical improvement projects, the M/PCpS Methodology also provides a very clearly defined step-by-step approach. The non-technical methodology is aimed at improving the administrative, service and transactional processes. By virtually eliminating or reducing defects, errors and mistakes the processes achieve Six Sigma Performance capability.

The M/PCpS Methodology for non-technical processes is similarly divided into five progressive stages:

Stage 1: Process Delineation
Stage 2: Measurement Generation
Stage 3: Performance Determination
Stage 4: Structured Gap Minimization
Stage 5: Monitoring & Total Control

The stages bring a structured order to the use of methods, tools and statistics from beginning to end. Every stage defines milestones to be reached by the teams involved in the improvement projects. The purpose of the methodology is to bring an objective and scientific approach to non-technical improvement projects and to include metrics, risk and confidence in decision-making.

Stage 1: Process Delineation

This involves defining the process and its sub-processes, its boundaries, elements, relations and their interactions, and, its response (input) and output variables. Decomposable mapping is used to obtain a macro and micro view of the process.

Stage 2: Measurement Generation

The measurement system needed to gauge the output variables and quantify the concordance of the measurement scales is defined. Likert scales may be produced, including descriptive sensory analysis and scoring and ranking methods, depending on the complexity of the responses under study. Other methods such as benchmarking and customer satisfaction analysis may be required in this stage.

Stage 3: Performance Determination

It is now necessary to determine the current ability of the (Administrative, Service or Transactional) process to provide the service within Six Sigma performance capability by establishing the gap between the response-matrix performance and the goals. All parametric and non-parametric descriptive statistics are calculated at this stage.

Stage 4: Structured Gap Minimization

Improving (closing) the gap that exists between the goal (Six Sigma) and the response-matrix reference is the next objective. Through planning, designing, testing and analyzing the possibilities (ideas, theories or hypothesis) the processes will be fixed, corrected or improved and the gap minimized. Experimentation assisted by possibility analysis, regression analysis and cost/benefit analysis are used in this stage.

Stage 5: Monitoring & Total Control

Finally, it is necessary to monitor the system for compliance to improvement targets, anticipate deterioration and establish controls and procedures to maintain Six Sigma Performance capability and total customer satisfaction. From the conclusion of the project, policy, standardization and documentation are established and maintained.

VII. Advanced Systems Consultants

Who is Advanced Systems Consultants?

ASC provides world-class consulting and training in Six Sigma and Variation Reduction programs for both manufacturing and service organizations. ASC was the first consulting firm to successfully provide Six Sigma training and services. It is also the exclusive provider of M/PCpS, the methodology used to achieve and sustain Six Sigma performance levels.

ASC's breakthrough five-stage M/PCpS Methodology for Process Characterization, Optimization and Control, delivers the most powerful step-by-step approach to superior quality and continuous process improvement. The M/PCpS Methodology was used internally at Motorola and was disseminated to team members so all would contribute to characterizing and optimizing their processes to Six Sigma levels.

ASC was founded in 1986 to provide training and consulting services and distribute the M/PCpS Methodology. In 1991, Mario Perez-Wilson resigned his position as Division Statistical Methods Engineering Manager at Motorola, to pioneer the implementation of M/PCpS for the achievement of Six Sigma at Allied Signal and other clients.

Six Sigma Quality Program

ASC is dedicated to helping organizations embark on and realize a Six Sigma Quality Program. The principal consultant, Mario Perez-Wilson, was Division Engineering Manager for the Statistical Methods Department at Motorola Inc. and developed the M/PCpS Methodology for making processes Six Sigma.

Variation Reduction Program

ASC excels at designing, customizing and implementing an organization-wide program for applying statistical principles for reduction of variability to achieve high levels of performance capability and quality. ASC has the knowledge and experience to make such a program successful in your organization.

Team Facilitation

Six Sigma performance requires guiding, coaching and leading teams in problem solving. Such teams must target the reduction of variability by implementing statistical methods and methodologies. ASC has world-wide experience in this field.

Customization

Every organization is unique and different. It is important to be capable of tailoring training courses to specific customers' needs, technologies, processes and problems. ASC recognizes this capability as a paramount principle in the services it provides.

Design of Methodologies

ASC can use its expertise in statistical methods to research and select the right array of tools and methods for the design and development of custom-made methodologies for use in specific industries, applications and complex problems.

Who is Mario Perez-Wilson?

Mario Perez-Wilson is the founder and principal consultant of Advanced Systems Consultants. He is the author of six books:
- The Machine/Process Characterization Study - A Five Stage Methodology for Optimizing Processes
- Multi-vari Chart and Analysis - A Pre-experimentation Technique

- Design of Experiments - A Seven Stage Methodology
- The Total Control Methodology - A Preventive Approach for Total Control during Production
- Positrol Plans and Logs
- Six Sigma - Understanding the Concept, Implications and Challenges

Mr. Perez-Wilson was Division Statistical Methods Engineering Manager at Motorola. During his tenure, he was successful in institutionalizing and standardizing the application of statistical methods in Motorola's worldwide manufacturing, production and engineering disciplines. His M/PCpS™ Methodology for characterizing manufacturing processes has received global recognition and has become the de facto standard in the achievement of Six Sigma Quality. In fact, it has been successfully implemented in the automotive, electronics, defense, medical, missile, pharmaceutical and semiconductor industries, and in Fortune 500 companies, all around the world.

Mr. Perez-Wilson has conducted training for over 10,000 individuals in Belgium, China, Hong Kong, India, Japan, Korea, Malaysia, Mexico, Philippines, Puerto Rico, Singapore, Taiwan, Thailand and the United States. He has consulted, trained, and implemented his methodologies in numerous companies around the world.

Mr. Perez-Wilson, who holds a B.S. degree in Systems & Industrial Engineering from the University of Arizona, was awarded the "Da N To Tsu" (Japanese for "Best of the Best") award from the Rochester Institute of Technology in the QED 90 Symposium. He is currently listed in The International

Who's Who in Quality.

Advanced Systems Consultants' Accomplishments

These are some of the companies which have benefitted from ASC's M/PCpS Methodology for achieving Six Sigma:

Motorola Government Electronics Group

In 1985 through 1987 Mario Perez-Wilson acting as coordinator of Statistical Methods trained and implemented the Process Characterization methodology in the FMU-139 electronic bomb fuze program. The first organization where the M/PCpS Methodology was implemented. The success of the implementation increased yields of over Six Sigma performance levels to the program and total record sales of over $263,000,000. In 1988, this unit of the Tactical Electronics Division received the Quality Excellence Award from ASQC for outstanding achievement in the use and implementation of statistical tools. In 1990, the FMU Fuze Program won the Chief Executive Office Quality Award (CEO Award), Motorola's highest award for quality performance.

In 1987, Mario Perez-Wilson as Staff Quality Engineer and still acting as coordinator of statistical methods, implemented the M/PCpS Methodology into the FZU-48 Bomb Fuze Initiator from the design stages all the way to Full Scale Production. After the completion of the first 115 deliverable FZU-48 units, an unforeseen design flaw resulted in failure of the First Article Acceptance Test. Aggressive utilization of

Statistically Designed Experiments corrected the problem. In a period of five weeks, fourteen consecutive statistically designed experiments were conducted, leading to product redesign changes and reduction of product performance variability, far exceeding Motorola's Six Sigma design objectives. Since production began in early August, 1987, the FZU-48 program increased its production 1100% per day and during this period of eight Lot Acceptance Tests not a single unit failed.

Motorola Malaysia Electronics - ISMF Fab

This Integrated Semiconductor Manufacturing Facility, located in Seremban, Malaysia, was the first wafer fabrication (Fab) in Seremban. It was also the first facility in Asia-Pacific to receive training on the implementation of M/PCpS in 1988. Every process and equipment and tool, went through a complete characterization and optimization in the subsequent years. In one particular process, Emitter Diffusion, the hFE variation led to electrical rejects at class probe quantified to have a $Cp=0.7$ and $Cpk=0.2$. After undergoing M/PCpS study, the variation was reduced, leading to a $Cp=2.6$ and $Cpk=2.2$, with estimated savings of over $40,000 annually.

Motorola de Mexico, S.A. - Guadalajara

This Motorola site was trained in Spanish on the M/PCpS Methodology by Mario Perez-Wilson in 1989. A site coordinator was identified and trained for six months in Phoenix, Arizona. The site launched Six Sigma by characterizing and optimizing its processes. Eduardo Bustamante, the site coordinator, later became a Statistical Methods Engineer responsible for coordinating all efforts to bring the site to Six Sigma performance capability. In the years that followed, Advanced Systems Consultants continued its training and consulting efforts with this site. On September 12, 1994, the Vice President General Manager, K. Kanapathi extended a Certificate of Recognition to Mario Perez-Wilson for ASC's excellent performance in developing his people in DOEx and Multi-vari Analysis.

Motorola Telcarro de Puerto Rico Inc.

In 1994, energized by the new Vice-President and General Manager, Omar Villareal, the Motorola plant in Puerto Rico embarked seriously on a Six Sigma Quality Program. The whole organization was trained in Six Sigma and the M/PCpS Methodology in Spanish by Advanced Systems Consultants. The synergy produced in that organization led to a full implementation such that most processes were characterized. and optimized to Six Sigma levels. A year later, Motorola Electronica de Puerto Rico, Inc. underwent the training to improve its pagers and cellular battery operations.

Motorola Electronics Pte. Ltd. - Ang Mo Kio

This Asia Pacific Paging Subscriber Division initiated a strong practice of M/PCpS in 1991. A single Site Coordinator was named and a number of teams started as they underwent a strong training program in M/PCpS process characterization.

Motorola Electronics (PCB Operations) Pte. Ltd. - Tuas

In 1994, soon after Motorola had opened a new operation to manufacture Printed Circuit Boards in Tuas, Singapore, Advanced Systems Consultants was brought in to disseminate the M/PCpS Methodology for Six Sigma. All their processes were characterized and optimized at the beginning stages of productions.

Motorola Electronics Pte. Ltd. - Pioneer

In 1995, Advanced Systems Consultants was also invited to train and deploy its M/PCpS Methodology in this new Printed Circuit Board facility. From the very beginning, they started implementing Six Sigma and characterized every process.

Motorola Malaysia Sdn. Bhd. - Kuala Lumpur

From 1988 through 1991, this campus of the Semiconductor Product Sector received training and implementation support from Mario Perez-Wilson as internal consultant to Motorola. Over four site coordinators were trained to support the successful implementation of Process Characterization and Six Sigma. A Manufacturing Center of Excellence was also established, and in 1991, they received the Chief Executive Office Quality Award.

Motorola Korea Ltd. - Seoul

Starting in 1988 this facility embarked on Six Sigma with training and implementation of M/PCpS. Two Site Coordinators were selected and trained. These individuals facilitated and guided teams in the implementation of the characterization program on a multitude of studies and projects. In 1991 a Process Capability Improvement team studying the Towa Molding Process were awarded the CEO Quality Award.

Motorola Semiconductor Hong Kong Ltd.- Hong Kong

Starting in 1989 the Hong Kong organization of Motorola also embarked on M/PCpS to achieve and sustain Six Sigma performance capability. In the deployment of the methodology teams were trained and two full time site coordinators were also selected and trained to manage the program. An SPS Manufacturing Center of Excellence was established and, in 1991, they were recognized with the CEO Quality Award.

Motorola Semiconductor Sdn. Bhd. - Seremban

This facility of the Semiconductor Product Sector in Seremban, Malaysia was trained by Mario Perez-Wilson starting in 1988 through 1991. Site coordinators were identified, trained and made responsible for deploying the Process Characterization program to achieve and sustain Six Sigma performance capability. A Manufacturing Center of Excellence was created in Seremban, and in 1991, they won the CEO

Six Sigma
output

Quality Award.

Motorola Asia Limited - Philippines

In 1990 the organization in Manila embarked on M/PCpS as the vehicle to achieve Six Sigma. Starting with Mario Perez-Wilson launching the program in 1990, site coordinators were developed to manage the efforts. The Philippines was also a site for the formation of a Manufacturing Center of Excellence and, in 1991, it received Motorola's highest award for quality performance.

Motorola Electronics Taiwan, Ltd.

In the Semiconductor Product Sector in Taiwan, two Statistical Methods Engineers were trained to coordinate all site activities for Six Sigma. The organization received training and consulting services in 1989 by Mario Perez-Wilson, then Division Engineering Manager of Statistical Methods Department.

In 1995, the Quartz Product Division and the Component Product Division in Chung-li, requested Advanced System Consultants to deploy the M/PCpS Methodology in support of the Six Sigma achievement.

Motorola (Advanced Messaging Group) - Ft. Worth

In 1997, as this Motorola Group expanded its production and assembly, it requested Advanced Systems Consultants to train their personnel in ASC's methodology for process characterization and optimization.

• 298 •
output

Motorola Lighting, Inc. - Illinois

In 1994, Jack Welch, CEO of General Electric wrote in his letter to GE's Share Owners about the new products introduced to the market. A major product introduction was a GE/Motorola-brand electronic fluorescent ballast. Advanced Systems Consultants was requested to assist Motorola Lighting in their quest for Six Sigma in this new venture. In 1995, the M/PCpS Methodology was implemented to characterize every single process and equipment. In 1998, Advanced Systems Consultants deployed the Total Control Methodology, TCM, to established a complete system of process control.

Motorola (Microcontroller Technologies Group) - Ed Bluestein

In 1993 and 1994, the Austin assembly operations also implemented Process Characterization as taught by Advanced Systems Consultants in Motorola's pursuit for Six Sigma quality. Processes, such as C4 BGA process, were characterized; these included equipment such as underfill dispensing systems, wafer dicing, pick-and-place, C4 placement, RTC furnaces, flux cleaners, screen printers and ball placement equipment.

Motorola (Microprocessor Products Group) - Oak Hill

From 1991 through 1994 Advanced System Consultants was involved in training and consulting the Microprocessor and Memory Technology Group in the methodology to achieve Six

Sigma. The ASECO supplier of Handlers was concurrently trained in characterizing their handlers to optimize their capability.

Motorola (P) Ltd. - India

This new site of the Pager Product Group in Bangalore, India, initiated its operations in 1994. In the same year, Advanced Systems Consultants was requested to kick off this Motorola Group's efforts towards Six Sigma. The M/PCpS Methodology was deployed to optimize their operations.

Motorola Malaysia (Penang) Sdh. Bhd.

The organization in the Malaysian island of Penang was also trained in 1993 in the M/PCpS Methodology as it embarked on its quest to achieve Six Sigma by characterizing and optimizing every process.

Motorola (China) Electronics Ltd.

The organization in Tianjin was trained on Six Sigma M/PCpS in 1994 as it was growing in their production of pagers and cellular phones. The year before, a significant portion of the Motorola's growth was in the People's Republic of China/Hong Kong operations. Total sales were $1.56 billion for both countries.

Motorola Paging Products Group - Boynton Beach

In 1994, the Paging Product Group - which designs,

manufactures and distributes a variety of messaging products including pagers - in Boynton Beach, Florida entered into a contract with ASC to deliver the M/PCpS Methodology for achieving Six Sigma.

Arvin North America Automotive Inc.

Starting in 1992, Arvin N.A. Automotive, which operates one of the world's most extensive technical centers dedicated solely to research and development of exhaust systems, underwent an implementation of M/PCpS to characterize all their processes.

A.N.A.A is a leading manufacturer of original equipment automotive exhaust systems, including mufflers, exhaust and tail pipes, catalytic converters, fuel filler tubes and small diameter tubing products. Over three thousand equipment and processes were characterized in processes such as, tube benders, sizers, notchers, welders, hydraulic presses, mechanical presses, dickey spinners, heater, muffler lock seamer, vertical, as well as horizontal, muffler spinners, wrappers, baffle rams, head rams, flare presses, end formers, miter cutters, robot welders, robot painters, plasma cutters, tube mills, doall saws, slitters, milling machines, seam solders, brazing furnaces and metallizers. This diverse variety of processes constituted a strong challenge to the robustness of the M/PCpS Methodology.

Allied Signal, Inc.

From 1990 to 1993, over 1400 individuals throughout Allied Signal were trained in ASC's M/PCpS Methodology to achieve Six Sigma. Allied Signal was the first company to undergo Six Sigma after Motorola. Starting in 1990, ASC was contracted to train the first round of Allied Signal Aerospace's Executives, Managers and Engineers at its Kansas City Division - including the President, VP and their staffs.

Maremont Exhaust Products, Inc.

In 1993, the leading manufacturer of replacement automotive exhaust products and inventor of the mechanical lock and the torque and spiral lock for exhaust products, also underwent a program of process characterization and optimization with Advanced Systems Consultants.

Arvin Ride Control, Inc.

In 1996, Arvin Ride Control Products, a leading manufacturer of ride control products and shock absorbers, embarked on ASC's M/PCpS program for process characterization and optimization.

Burr-Brown Corporation

Burr-Brown is a leading designer and manufacturer of analog and mixed-signal integrated circuits, which translate analog signals from pressure, temperature, speed and sound into digital signals and vice versa. Starting in 1990, it has relied on ASC for various sessions of M/PCpS training.

Advanced Micro Devices, Inc.

In 1994, as the installation of equipment for its new Fab25 - with 86,700 square feet of Class 1 clean room - AMD requested ASC train its people in M/PCpS, so they could start characterizing their processes and equipment. Fab 25 is among the world's most cost-effective semiconductor facilities with a production capacity of over 5,000 eight-inch wafers per week.

General Electric Company

Starting in 1992, sponsored by the Sandia National Laboratories, Advanced Systems Consultants was brought into GE Aerospace to institute a comprehensive system to fully characterize machines, process and metrology. The first process studied in a classroom setting was a flame sprayer robot in generator potting and preparation.

ADFlex Solutions Inc.

Early 1998, ADFlex Solutions, one of the largest manufacturers of flexible interconnects in the USA, and among the largest in the world, embarked on Six Sigma. In the first nine months of implementation of M/PCpS to achieve Six Sigma, the defect levels were brought down by 50%.

Anadigics

In 1997, Anadigics, who fabricates radio-frequency and microwave integrated circuits from gallium arsenide, embarked on characterizing, optimizing and controlling their processes in their GaAs wafer fabs. An extensive utilization of M/PCpS characterization was made in their facilities. Anadigics has delivered over 80 million GaAs ICs and was the first GaAs IC manufacturer to receive ISO-9000 Certification.

Bausch & Lomb, Inc.

A leading maker of premium sunglasses, including their famous Ray-Ban, Porsche-Design and Killer Loop brands, initiated in 1993 a long term program for characterizing and optimizing all their processes in their facilities in Rochester, New York, Oakland, Maryland and San Antonio, Texas. Advanced Systems Consultants' M/PCpS Methodology was used in all of these facilities.

Sandia National Laboratories

From 1990 to 1992 Sandia National Labs, the national security laboratory which designs all non-nuclear components for the USA's nuclear weapons, contracted ASC to provide training and consulting in the M/PCpS Methodology. As an assurance that the M/PCpS Methodology was statistically sound, Sandia required the first session be taught to their Phd Statisticians for their evaluation.

Ryobi Outdoor Products

Well known for their world's lightest hand held 4-cycle engine, and makers of lawn and garden equipment sold under the Ryobi brand, as well as by Sears under the Craftsman brand name, underwent training in M/PCpS in 1998, in their quest for world-class excellence.

Vitelic Hong Kong Ltd.

As Motorola Inc. entered into an agreement to transfer its proprietary TMOS wafer processing technology to Mosel Vitelic, Advanced Systems Consultants was brought in to train the wafer fabrication plant in Hong Kong. Vitelic Hong Kong Ltd. wafer fab underwent TMOS wafer technology transfer, certification and complete training in M/PCpS and Six Sigma before its planned production by mid-1997.

ASC's Clients

- ADFlex Solutions
- Advanced Micro Devices
- Alliance Technologies
- Alphatec U.S.A.
- Allied Signal Aerospace
- Anadigics
- Arvin Industries
- Arvin North America Automotive
- Arvin Ride Controls
- Bausch & Lomb
- Burr-Brown Corporation
- Carsem
- EG&G
- CTI Cryogenics
- Duracell
- Fiberite IBI

- General Electric Aerospace
- Hewlett Packard
- Indy Electronics
- Intel Corp.
- Korea Electronic Company
- LSI Logic
- Lucas/Nova Sensors
- Maremont Exhaust Products
- Martin Marietta Astronautics
- Mitsubishi Silicon America
- Motorola Inc.
- Olin Interconnect Technologies
- Pacesetter
- Rodel
- Ryobi Outdoor Products
- Sandia National Laboratories
- Semi-Alloys
- Shimano
- Sikorsky Aircraft
- Vitelic (Hong Kong) Ltd.
- Zimmer Inc.

ASC's Client Endorsements

"What makes Advanced Systems Consultants stand out from the crowd is the pro-active approach their methodology uses. I have now implemented ASC's methodology, tools and techniques in three different companies with the same dramatic results each time. First at Motorola, then at Alphatec and now at ADFlex Solutions this methodology has brought an in depth process knowledge which reduces scrap and makes processes much more robust. In the latest implementation here at ADFlex we have reduced scrap by 54% in the last 9 months and we are just getting started! This improved process efficiency is leading to shorter cycle times and smoother introduction of new designs."

Neil Dial
CEO
ADFlex Solutions, Inc.

"Mario Perez-Wilson's five-stage M/PCpS Methodology for optimizing manufacturing processes can provide the foundation for Motorola's Six Sigma initiative."

U.J. Jadunandan
Automation Engineer
Motorola Inc.

"Excellent and inclusive presentation of the procedure to attain processes that meet and maintain the high quality standards required (demanded) of business today."

Bruce Bowles
Process Engineer
GE Neutron Devices Department

"I believe that this process will allow a method of improvement based on facts related to the process and change the old myth that product problems are mostly related to the operator."

W. J. Ausmer
Manufacturing Superintendent
Allied Signal Inc.

"I have taken classes with Deming and Montgomery but this

class was by far the best. Mario's approach is very simple and practical."

David Butler
Director of Package Operations
Olin Interconnect

"M/PCpS Methodology is an extremely well planned, step-by-step course on 'how to' design, plan and complete [characterization] studies. Most seminars that I have attended are predominately theory with very little applications. The instructor's experience and knowledge was excellent and made the seminar extremely enjoyable. Probably the BEST seminar I have ever attended - approximately ten in the last three years."

Jim Angel
Director Manufacturing Quality
Arvin NAA

"Your presentation of the M/PCpS Methodology came across as clear, concise, logical, sequential, and self-documenting. I consider this methodology to be a valuable tool for analysis of complex problems. I enjoyed the course."

Jim Cates
SMTS Industrial Engineer
SNL

"The real genius of the M/PCpS Methodology is that it ties together and organizes all the tools for process improvement. I've taken many courses on S.P.C. and process improvement that have presented one piece of the puzzle, but none of the courses have put it all together as well as what Mario does in the M/PCpS course. This is by far the best training course I have taken."

Brian Decker
Senior Quality Engineer
Martin Marietta

"I have attended several SPC courses from, Six Sigma, DOE and Designed for Manufacturability. This is by far the best course in Process Characterization. Great combination of theory and practice."

Juan Cotto
TPM Advisor
Intermedics Orthopedics

"I liked the seminar very much. I only wish more companies would use it. I think it's what it will take for the U.S. to grow. I think the M/PCpS Methodology is what America needs."

John A. Gibbs
Product Engineer
McKenzie Technology

"Mario's M/PCpS program represents a practical and easy to follow approach to PC&C. Implementation of the techniques taught in this course is key to the survival of the American manufacturing industry."

Gary Grissum
Staff Engineer
Allied Signal Inc.

"M/PCpS provided an outstanding and integrated overview of practical statistical methods and a clear direction for applying the methodologies to foster a 'take control' approach ...

Education in their methods and actual application of them is now critical for American companies to 'close the gap'."

Scott P. Gucciardi
QA Engineer
Welch Allyn Corp.

"The information and methods shared in this seminar are crucial if today's manufacturing companies are to remain competitive. A continuous improvement culture is not possible without a clear, well-defined system."

Brett A. Jones
Senior Engineer
Allied Signal Inc. Aerospace

"The most comprehensive process control class I have attended. Combines many of today's single applications to the total process of quality control."

Corey Jones
Senior Project Engineer
Sikorsky Aircraft

"This course is a must... Mario Perez-Wilson presents his material in an eloquent fashion, displaying his experience, knowledge, and expertise. This was the most concise and comprehensive course I've taken for Process Improvement Methodologies."

Ron Koronkowski
Quality Assurance Engineer
Ventritex, Inc.

"Many people have presented these techniques in many other

seminars. Mario Perez-Wilson has significantly added value by organizing these techniques into a workable methodology and demonstrating how it can be applied to produce the desired results."

George Melchiorsen
Quality Engineer
Hewlett Packard

"Use of SPC is the way to keep our leadership in high-tech marketplace and to have a methodology and/or system such as the one developed by Advanced Systems Consultants which has all the elements is a winner."

Siroos Mirzadeh
Section Manager, Assembly Engineering
LSI Logic Corporation

"The M/PCpS Methodology is very systematically done, easy to understand and apply."

Tan Swee Lim
Manufacturing Engineer
Hewlett Packard Singapore Pte. Ltd.

"Very systematic approach in the M/PCpS study. The most beneficial knowledge gained is how to use the statistical tools logically and systematically. Very good! ..."

Chea Kar Lin
Process Engineer
AT&T Consumer Product Pte. Ltd.

"....a very systematic approach to machine and/or process characterization study, which guides the student all the way from the start of the problem to the end—forming positrol plans and control charts, to sustain manufacturing excellence."

A. K. Mah
Senior Process Engineer
Motorola Penang

"Mario has put together a very easy to use methodology that can yield results quickly and easily. This is something that can be used effectively..."

Ken Kennedy
Staff Engineer
Allied Signal Inc. Aerospace

"Very clear, concise explanation of difficult concepts and techniques. Examples and exercises have helped to improve understanding. A practical methodology!"

Lee Chat Guan
TQC Administration Manager
Texas Instruments (S) Pte. Ltd.

"Good, practical approach to tackling difficult manufacturing problems. Good class notes, and straightforward, concise approach."

Stephen V. Crowder
Senior Member Technical Staff
Sandia National Labs

"This course helped me to carry out a process characterization study in a better logical manner which top management would understand."

Alan Foley

Quality Customer Service Manager
Peak Plastic

"An extremely structured and step-by-step methodology -very clear and simplified. I strongly recommend all personnel involved in production or manufacturing at all levels to attend this seminar if they are really serious about improving their product quality."

Norman Sim Boon Heng
SPC Analyst
Sundstrand Pacific (Atg) P.L.

"M/PCpS is a clear Methodology for step-by-step process characterization and is one of the most important tools any process engineer can weld to ensure total control of the process."

Jaikishan G.
Process Engineer
Motorola (P) Ltd. ,

"This methodology should be a requirement of all engineers BEFORE they begin a new job out of school. Knowing the M/PCpS Methodology will save their company lots of money and valuable engineering time."

Dina Kraft
Process Development Engineer
Motorola, Inc.

"Finally, someone can explain the 'why' of what we have to do. It's all here in one place. Thanks, Mario, for a great book and course. I wish we had someone like you at LSI to look over my shoulder. This course is the next best thing!"

Frank Fulton
Industrial Engineer
LSI Logic

"This book presents a very methodical and logical approach to not only processing control but also process capabilities. I feel like the points presented and the method will be very beneficial as our processes grow and become more complex"

Eric Farmer
Industrial Engineer
Rodel Inc.

"A very well structured course and an excellent methodology. The worksheets have also been very well designed and thought out. The M/PCpS course is well recommended to all who are serious about quality improvements in our production lines across Motorola."

A. A. Do Rego
Sr. Production Administrator
Motorola (P) Ltd.

"I think you did an excellent job and truly respect your ability to teach as well as relate this vital tool to a broad spectrum of individuals. Thanks for sharing your expertise and knowledge. This is the best course of actual hands-on use of SPC data for the real world. The instructor is excellent in both the area of presentation and knowledge. His ability to take a sophisticated science and make it applicable as well as comprehensible for the average person places him 'head and shoulders' above the others..."

Kurt A. Hutchings

Business Unit Manager
Arvin Industries

"... Mario, in his book M/PCpS, has produced a system which prevents the costly redundancies in product/process development and focuses an Engineering structure to encompass the techniques of experimental design and communicate results that infuse quality in products, processes and services."

Thomas B. Barker
Associate Professor - CQAS
Rochester Institute of Technology

"Method [M]
 Provides [P]
 Continuous [C]
 profits [p]
 Success [S]
For any organization, M/PCpS provides the above!"

Devprasad
Equipment Engineer
Motorola (P) Ltd.

Six Sigma Courses

Six Sigma Executive Overview

This Executive Overview presents the importance of reducing variation, defects and errors in all the processes throughout an organization in order to increase market share, minimize costs and increase profit margins. Strong emphasis is placed on explaining the Six Sigma Breakthrough Model and implementation of the M/PCpS Methodology for reduction of variability and achievement of Six Sigma.

Executives will develop an excellent understanding of how variation, defects and error reduction and process characterization affect product and service quality, performance, productivity and costs as well as the essential elements necessary to deploy a Six Sigma effort throughout the organization.

Achieving Six Sigma

This course teaches the participants the philosophy of Six Sigma and how to achieve that level of excellence in an organization. It covers the basics for understanding the meaning of sigma, and the concepts behind Six Sigma. This includes its computation, derivation from the Normal Distribution and other distributions, and its function as an index of quality and excellence.

The course demonstrates the role of Six Sigma as a quality goal and its measurements associated to other indices, such as Process Capability Indices (Cp, Cpk, Cpm), Parts-per-million (PPM), Defects-per-million (DPM), Defects-per-million-opportunities (DPMO). It discuses the controversies behind ± 1.5 sigma shift, 3.4 part-per-million defective versus 2 parts-per-billion defective and the true meaning of ± 6 sigma. A road map showing how to reduce variability, defects and errors and achieve Six Sigma in both technical (manufacturing) and non-technical (administrative, service and transactional) processes is also presented.

The M/PCpS Methodology for Achieving Six Sigma

This course teaches the participants a five-stage methodology for characterizing and improving technical and non-technical processes to bring them to Six Sigma performance capability.

The M/PCpS Methodology sets the order and approach of how processes should be optimized to fulfill total customer satisfaction, i.e., reduce variability, eradicate defects, errors, and mistakes, reduce scrap and costs, and streamline the process by eliminating non-value-added steps, minimizing cycle time and increasing accuracy and efficiency.

VIII. Frequently Asked Questions

Frequently Asked Questions (FAQs)

What is Sigma?

Sigma is a Greek letter signifying the parameter of the Normal Distribution. This parameter is the standard deviation of the population. Sigma or the standard deviation is conceptually the average deviation of the data from its mean. The smaller the sigma, the less variability the data has, and the larger the sigma, the more variability there is in the data.

The most important point to remember is the smaller the value of sigma, the better the process.

The sigma, is a funny parameter. By itself, when we look at its value, it is difficult to visualize what it really means, so, usually the sigma is compared against something else, such as another sigma, a tolerance or specification limits.

What is Six Sigma?

Six Sigma is an optimized level of performance approaching zero-defects in a process producing a product or service. It is a statistic, a metric, a strategy, a goal, a benchmark, a vision, and a philosophy. It indicates achievement and maintenance of world-class performance. Six Sigma is not a methodology. It is an end not a means.

Why a Cpk of 2.0 for Six Sigma?

A process is said to be Six Sigma, when its variability (process width) is equal to one half the specification width (difference between the USL minus the LSL). If the process average is centered in the middle of the specification limits, and the process variability is equal to one half of the specification width, then the Cpk would be equal to 2.0 and also equal to the Cp. The minimum Cpk for a Six Sigma process is a Cpk=2, the Cp could be much greater than 2.0.

How is Six Sigma measured?

Six Sigma is measured by collecting data and converting it into various forms: a particular characteristic average and standard deviation, defects, errors or mistakes, Cp, Cpk, dpu, dpm, ppm, epu, epm, DPMO, and EPMO. To characterize and optimize a process it is necessary to measure or quantify it by collecting data and by summarizing these data into indices, metrics or statistics.

What is a standard deviation?

The standard deviation is a statistic showing the lack of uniformity in a data set in relation to its average. The more scattered the data are with respect to its average, the more variability or lack of uniformity the data has. On the other hand, the more clustered the data are around its average, the more uniformity there is. The smaller the value of the standard deviation, the better or more uniform the process.

Do you need statistics to implement Six Sigma?

There is a definite need to understand statistics, but there is no need to be an expert. Generally, a stronger understanding of applied statistics is needed to implement Six Sigma in technical processes than in non-technical processes. The application of statistics has been simplified tremendously by the use of tables, forms, and worksheets, many of which are supported by computers and software in everyday use.

Why do I need a methodology to achieve Six Sigma?

A methodology to achieve Six Sigma focuses on reducing or eliminating the incidence of errors, defects and mistakes in a process. It also aims at reducing the variability of the process and its characteristics, eventually improving the product or service provided by the process. A methodology for achieving Six Sigma does this by characterizing, optimizing and controlling the process. The methodology is a process approach, and the approach to it, is itself a process, with many possible iterations of applications in many industries, companies and processes.

Who uses a methodology to achieve Six Sigma?

Motorola was the first company to start Six Sigma in 1987. Soon after that, Allied Signal followed suit by training over 1400 people. Advanced Systems Consultants provided training in its M/PCpS Methodology to Allied Signal from 1990 through 1993. Allied Signal was later followed by Sandia National Laboratories, Burr-Brown, General Electric, Martin Marrieta, LSI Logic and Arvin Industries, who started training in ASC's M/PCpS Methodology in 1992.

In what industries can Six Sigma be used?

Six Sigma can be used in almost all industries. It is currently used in the aerospace industry by Allied Signal; in banking and finance by GE Capital; in consumer products by Shimano; in electronics by ADFlex Solutions, Chartered Semiconductor and Motorola; in the medical industry by Mayo Health Care; in the paper industry by Avery Dennison; in trans-

portation by the US Post Office; and the list just keeps on growing.

Where does the name Six Sigma come from?

The term "Six Sigma" comes from Motorola's Six
Sigma Quality Program launched in January, 1987.

Is it necessary to be a high volume operation to achieve Six Sigma?

Not at all. This is probably the biggest misconception
about Six Sigma. Whether you are producing a few missiles in
a month or a half a ton of semiconductor silicone die in a
month, Six Sigma can be implemented to quantify and optimize
the level of performance capability.

What indices do we need to track?

The most typical indices tracked are:
Cp - Process potential index
Cpk - Process Capability Index
FPY - First pass yield
dpm - defects per million
epm - errors per million
ppm - parts per million defective
DPMO - defects per million opportunities
EPMO - errors per million opportunities

There are more industry specific indices referred to as Six Sigma performance indices, such as:

On-time Delivery

Process Yield

Assembly Yield

Customer Returns

What are the benefits of achieving Six Sigma performance?

The benefits of embarking on and achieving Six Sigma are multiple:

Change in culture

Establishing a common language and
methods for improvements

Simplification of processes

Reduce defects

Reduce scrap

Reduce rework

Reduce errors

Reduce mistakes

Cycle-time improvements

Bottom-line improvements

Market share improvement

Profitability improvement

What does achieving Six Sigma mean?

Achieving Six Sigma means reducing defects, errors or

mistakes to zero-defects and/or reducing the sigma or standard deviation to a value that will allow you to fit twelve times the value of sigma between the upper and lower specification limits, while having the average as close as possible to the middle of the specification.

Do we need a full-time person for Six Sigma?

Full-time Site Coordinators may be needed, depending on the size of the organization. And, depending on the number of studies and projects, full-time Team Leaders may be necessary as well. A Site Coordinator may supervise about ten Team Leaders, and a Team Leader may facilitate and manage successfully two teams.

A full-time position dedicated to bring about the Six Sigma cultural change in the organization and be involved in the studies and projects would definitively increase the success and financial rewards of the program.

Do we need to hire new personnel for Six Sigma?

Not particularly. The objective of attaining Six Sigma is to bring about a culture change in the organization, and to prepare employees to use a methodology proven successful in other companies. Such preparation does not consist of just training four people, but the entire organization, making them realize they have the power for improving quality. It is not about delegating quality away to just a few, or even to a few newly hired, and presumed experts. It is about teaching new methods, techniques, tools and metrics and about demonstrating how to use them to everyone, so everyone can understand the relevance of the methodology to the work they do.

Can we implement the methodology for attaining Six Sigma ourselves or do we need a consultant?

Of course you can do it yourself, but why expend precious energy and limited resources reinventing the wheel? In most cases, the consulting firm has already implemented a Six Sigma program in various organizations and you benefit from their experience and expertise. So you should concentrate on selecting an experienced consulting firm that has already lived it and not just a novice firm or one who uses someone else's materials.

Who trains us and in what tools?

Advanced Systems Consultants (ASC) has the experience in training the most diverse levels of individuals, from training Sandia National Laboratories the biggest congregation of PhD's and MS degrees in the world, to training small companies with as few as five engineers. ASC has trained individuals all over the world, in a variety of industries.

Can it be done piecemeal?

No, you cannot do it piecemeal. It doesn't make sense to choose and do only one part of the program and not the rest. It simply doesn't work. Attaining Six Sigma means bringing about a cultural change in an organization, and this cannot be done in one department at a time. It has to be done from the top down in a systematic fashion.

How long does it take?

Motorola in 1987 set a five year target to achieve Six Sigma. General Electric set itself a goal of becoming a Six Sigma quality company by the year 2000. This goal was established in 1996, when they initiated their full-blown commitment to Six Sigma. Again a five year target.

The initial training of the organization does not take but a few months. Within a few months, teams are already working on characterization studies and improvement projects.

The full deployment of the Six Sigma program and its tools, takes a few years. It is an intensive training that involves people from all levels of the organization. As they are trained and teams are formed, they are empowered - by the executive leaders - to apply these tools and methodology to characterize and optimize their processes. Every time a team does an iteration of using the methodology on a particular process, a process is improved to Six Sigma levels. The results are obtained at each iteration. How long (time) does it take for a company to achieve Six Sigma? It depends entirely on the number of people trained, the number of processes to be optimized and the number of iterations they make. The more iterations of the methodology, the more processes are elevated to Six Sigma, the more processes are at zero-defects, with no errors and mistakes. The rewards appear at every iteration.

Would your organization be able to achieve a Six Sigma level of quality? It all depends on the level of commitment of the organization, the number of people trained and the number of iterations you want them to make. Do you ever stop? Why would you want to stop. The purpose of the Six Sigma program is to ingrain this methodology into everybody's work ethic and make it the company's culture.

Do you ever reach Six Sigma? Of course, you reach Six Sigma in every process, product, service you apply the methodology.

How is attaining Six Sigma going to make us better?

Pursuit and achievement of Six Sigma entails use of a standard methodology to improve all the processes by eliminating defects, errors and mistakes and optimizing the processes, and its outputs. The optimization of the process dramatically improves quality, reduces waste, maximizes productivity and prompts significant cost savings.

What resources are needed?

Six Sigma improvements are achieved by characterizing and optimizing processes through the formation of teams. Team Leaders are necessary to manage these teams, which on average consist of seven individuals. Site Coordinators manage a group of about 10 Team Leaders. Team Leaders report indirectly to Champions or Team Mentors. Team Mentors have an average of two studies or projects and each study or project has the potential to bring $75,000 in cost improvements. The number of studies or projects depends on the organizations objectives.

How much will it cost?

It depends on a couple of factors: on the organization's current performance level in comparison to Six Sigma performance levels and on the commitment for achieving those levels.

For example, a Japanese client I visited a year ago, who has captured a market niche through excellence in design, research and outgoing product quality, had an interest in Six Sigma. If this market leader delivers an excellent outgoing quality in its product, but maintains a significant internal in-process scrap level, then this organization's "performance level of excellence" is still far from Six Sigma. Therefore, this market leader would need a strong level of commitment to bring its internal level of performance to Six Sigma.

In 1997, Jack Welch's commitment to Six Sigma efforts at GE required a $300 million expenditure to enjoy a $600 million benefit.

What are the roadblocks or problems we might encounter during Six Sigma implementation?

During the implementation of Six Sigma at one of our clients, we faced this same question and decided to facilitate a brainstorming session with all the Site Coordinators and these are the results summarized by the following five categories in an Ishikawa Diagram:

Machine
Operation
    Too much variability
    No procedures
    No standardization
Materials & Resources
    Not tracking quality
    Vendors changed
    No traceability
    No in-coming inspection
Maintenance
    Not done
    No history
    No schedule
    No procedure
    No parts replacement traceability
Process not under control

Equipment setup
  No qualification
  Not consistent
  No procedures
  Too time consuming
Process variables changing
  New dominating variables
  Vital few
  Trivial many
Equipment
  Needs operator assistance
  Too many breakdowns
  Poor efficiency
Changes made in process
  No accountability
  By engineering
  By operator
  No traceability

Manpower
Discipline
  Poor
  To build quality, avoid specification procedure
Don't know how to fix process
Training
  Assembly instructions
  Production instructions
  Inspection instructions
  Operation
  Not available
  Process qualification

Too infrequent

No education on product, customer & process
application

Engineering

Doesn't spend time in production area

Doesn't understand process

Doesn't experiment

Constantly changing the process

Operator

Not asked

Not listened to

Not trained

Not motivated

Not consistent in running process

Procedures

Non available

Not correct

Not followed

Not respected

Too technical

Difficult too follow

Measurement

No calibration plan

Collect data but not on right response

No GR&R plan

Defects

Reducing

Intermittent appearance

Gauges

Not reproducible

             Not accurate
             Not repeatable
             Not available
Response
             Don't understand
             Attribute type
Don't know what is critical

Materials
Materials not characterized
No in-coming inspection
             No sampling
Families of variation
             Not understood
             Not quantified
             Between-lot variability
             Within-lot variability
             Lot-to-lot changes
                  No control
Materials change
             No engineering study
             Based on cost
Inconsistent
Too much variation
Vendors
             Process not characterized
             Not under control
             Process changes w/o notice·
             Too much variability

Methods
No maintenance procedure
No inspection instruction
    No criteria for defects
Standardization (nonexistent or inconsistent)
    Between product lines
    Between machines
    Between shifts
    Between operators
    Between processes

Is Six Sigma another fad?

No, Six Sigma is not a fad. When done correctly, Six Sigma is a powerful program that works and brings significant improvements and excellence to an organization. However, the strong publicity that has been generated recently has prompted many organizations to initiate half-baked programs which are doomed to failure. And this market frenzy is also causing consulting firms to jump on the bandwagon without understanding the concepts, implications and challenges to run a successful program. All of this is giving it the appearance of a fad, but it is not, because Six Sigma benefits speak to the basics of business success: quality, productivity and cost.

How do we overcome resistance and achieve buy-in?

To overcome resistance and achieve buy-in, the change needs to be initiated at the top of the organization. The most crucial change in an organization to implement Six Sigma successfully is that the Management Leadership - the CEOs and their staff - be convinced and demand Six Sigma be the way of running their business.

As the top Executive Leadership leads the Six Sigma cultural change, the rest of management will follow, and it will trickle down to the employees involved in the administrative, service and manufacturing processes.

This is the ultimate lesson learned from implementing Six Sigma and, for that matter, any revolutionary change in an organization. CEOs must be the ultimate leaders in the Six Sigma program: Jack Welch does it for GE, Larry Bossidy does it for Allied Signal, and Bob Galvin did it in 1987 for Motorola.

What is a methodology?

A methodology is more than just a method - an orderly, logical or systematic way of accomplishing something. It is a logically, systematically and clearly organized set of tools, techniques, methods, principles and rules for use as a guide and a step-by-step approach to achieve something - something like the study, project, analysis or evaluation of a particular subject.

A sound methodology will provide a proven approach, a step-by-step procedure that can be easily followed by all. This means selecting the right methods, tools and techniques - and the proper formulations, when necessary - and, then, setting them in the right sequence and, finally, establishing the right set of rules and procedures.

What does M/PCpS stand for?

M/PCpS stands for Machine and Process Characterization Studies. It is a step-by-step methodology for characterizing processes, whether the process is an administrative, service or transactional or manufacturing process. M/PCpS is a trademark of Advanced Systems Consultants and Mario Perez-Wilson.

What is process characterization?

Process characterization is a study done to gain a full understanding of all the output or response variables, and their cause-and-effect relationship with all the input or independent variables in a process. The eventual objective of the study is to optimize the output variables by manipulating the input variables to the level that guarantees Six Sigma performance, closest to zero defects, errors and mistakes. In Total Process Characterization™, all characteristics are optimized to achieve a perfect product, or service.

Who developed the M/PCpS Methodology?

The M/PCpS Methodology was designed by Mario Perez-Wilson, merging his experience with applied statistics from his years with the Laboratory of Tree-Ring Research and engineering statistics in manufacturing. The methodology took from 1986 through 1988 to refine before he got a final recipe that could be applied to any process, whether the process was for producing semiconductor products, nuclear tubes, hospital beds, or the process was an administrative process such as answering telephone calls in a travel agency.

Can a small company use M/PCpS to achieve Six Sigma?

Absolutely, both Six Sigma and M/PCpS are relevant in small companies as well as in large organizations. The common misconception is that because Six Sigma and M/PCpS use statistics and indices involving parts-per-million, defects-per-million, or errors-per-million, users need to be doing things in millions, such as, producing a million identical products, or receiving a million telephone calls or a million transactions. That could not be further from the truth. The reason for using indices expressed in millions is to quantify the severity of the lack of quality and inefficiency and for these to be expressed in sigmas. Statistics is applicable whether producing only two RAH-66 Comanche Helicopters in a year or processing the admissions of 3,000 students per year at a university.

Why be concerned about Six Sigma performance if we're already doing SPC?

Statistical Process Control or SPC are tools to monitor or control a process, mainly technical processes, like a production process. Six Sigma performance goes beyond controlling a process. First, it goes after delineating it, characterizing its measurement system, determining its current performance and, based on that knowledge, it goes after improving it or optimizing it. Finally, it goes after monitoring process quality during production while controlling it. So, the control stage or SPC is really the final thing done to a process in a Six Sigma implementation program.

IX. Glossary of Terms

Glossary of Terms

Accuracy - The extent to which the average of a series of repeated measurements on a single response deviates from its true value. Also referred to as bias or error.

Analysis of variance - A statistical analysis by which the total variation of a set of data is subdivided into its components each of which is associated with a specific source of variation. Also referred to by its abbreviation ANOVA.

Assignable cause - Refers to the ability to identify a factor(s) that is(are) responsible for an effect detected which is not due to chance.

Attribute - A characteristic appraised in terms of whether it meets or does not meet a given qualitative requirement.

Examples: pass or fail, go or no go.

Average - The arithmetic mean.

Bias - See **Accuracy.**

Bell-shaped distribution - A type of distribution having the overall shape of a vertical cross section of a bell. A Normal or Gaussian distribution have this particular characteristic.

Binomial distribution - The distribution of the number of successes in n trials, when the probability of a success remains constant from trial-to-trial and the trials are independent.

Capability indices - Refers to various statistics (i.e.: Cp, Cpk and Cpm) which quantify process variability with respect to the specification tolerances.

Characteristic - A particular response of interest for measurement. Also referred to as a response variable, response, output or dependent variable.

Common cause - Refers to the ability to identify a factor(s) that is(are) responsible for an effect due only to chance.

Control - The ability to make something behave the way you want it to.

Control charts - Graphic method for evaluating whether a process is in a state of statistical control.

Control limits - Lines on a control chart that serve as a basis for judging whether a pattern is in a state of statistical control. Control limits are statistically derived and represent ± 3 sigma limits.

Corrective Action Log (CAL) - A traceability log on the back of control charts to record action taken when control charts exhibit lack of statistical control.

Cycle time - The elapsed time between the beginning and the end of a task.

Data - Facts or information or statistics obtained from direct observation or measurement.

Defect - A failure to meet a particular qualitative requirement imposed on a unit.

Defective - A unit, product or service containing at least one defect or having several imperfections which in combination cause the unit to fail to satisfy its intended use.

Dependent variable - A characteristic which is directly influenced by an independent variable. See **Response, Response variable** or **Characteristic.**

Design of Experiment (DOE) - A formal plan for conducting statistically designed experiments.

Dispersion - The degree of scatter shown by data pertaining to a characteristic.

Distribution - When referring to observed data, the term distribution is used to make reference to the over-all variability of the data. When referring to a random variable, the term distribution refers to the probability structure of the random variable as defined by its probability formula.

dpm - Defects per million, is the total number of defects we expect to find should we produce a million units. Computed by multiplying the dpu times one million.

dpu - Defects per unit, or the total number of defects expected to be found in a unit of product. Computed by taking the total number of defects found in a sample and dividing it by the sample size.

Effect - The change in response produced by a change in the level of the factor.

Experimental design - See **Design of experiment.**

Factor - A variable under investigation; usually, but not necessarily, an independent variable. See **Independent variable.**

Factorial design - An experimental design in which the levels of each factor are combined with all levels of every other factor.

F distribution - Is the variance-ratio distribution. It is of fundamental importance in analysis of variance.

Fraction defective - The total number of defective items divided by the total number of items.

Fractional factorial design - A factorial design in which not all combinations of the factors are tested.

Frequency distribution - An arrangement which shows the classes into which a set of data have been grouped together with the corresponding frequencies, that is, the number of items falling into each class.

Gauge R&R - Gauge repeatability and reproducibility are studies in which two sources of variation are quantified: variation due to the gauge (repeatability) and variation due to the operators (reproducibility).

Gauge - A measuring device used to measure characteristics in a product.

Histogram - A graph of a frequency distribution produced by vertical bars whose bases coincide with the class interval and whose heights are proportional to the frequency of occurrence.

Independent variable - A factor or random variable that can independently be set to different levels.

Inspection - The process of ascertaining the value of product or service characteristics or performance against a set of requirements.

Inspection 100% - Inspection of all the units in a lot or batch.

Inspection by attributes - An inspection in which the item is classified as either defective or non-defective (or conforming or nonconforming) or by the number of defects.

Inspection by variables - An inspection in which the item is evaluated with respect to a scale of measurements.

Key characteristics - A characteristic significant to customer requirements.

Level - The setting of a factor in an experiment.

Mean - The arithmetic mean commonly referred to as the average, and computed by adding n observations and dividing it by its sample size n.

Non-normal distribution - A distribution that does not follow the Normal or Gaussian distribution.

Normal distribution - Also referred to as the Gaussian distribution, the Normal distribution was first studied in connection with the occurrence of errors in measurements. Although the probability structure of the Normal distribution is defined by the Normal Probability function or formula, it can be summarized by most of the observations being around the mean, that is, those having the highest probability of occurring, and as the values deviate above and below the mean, their probability of occurrence starts diminishing towards zero, but never actually reaching zero.

Normal - Unless otherwise stated, refers to the property of being distributed in the form of a Normal distribution.

Out-of-control - Refers to a process shown by its control chart to exhibit lack of statistical control.

Out-of-control Action Plan (OCAP) - A document to advise production personnel on specific actions to be taken for specific out-of-control conditions when using control charts in a production process.

Population - The infinite set of values which can be assumed by a continuous random variable. Also referred to as the universe.

Positrol log - A traceability log to record control activities and information as specified by the Positrol plan.

Positrol plan - A positive control plan to monitor and control essential characteristics and variables of a process to maintain is stable, capable and fool-proof of defects.

Process potential index (Cp) - An index measuring the potential of capability of a process relative to its specification.

Precision - The tendency to have values cluster closely around the mean of its sampling distribution.

Probability - The chance of something happening.

Process average - The mean of a given characteristic in a process.

Process capability index (Cpk) - An index measuring the process variability relative to the process specification and the target.

Process variability - The distance from -3 sigma to +3 sigma in the frequency distribution curve of a particular process response. It is measured by multiplying 6 times the standard deviation. Also referred to as the process spread or process width.

Process width - See **Process variability.**

Probability distribution - A distribution of the relative frequencies of a random variable.

Response - It is an output; a variable or characteristic measured in a process. See **Dependent variable.**

Sample - A set of observations of size n from a larger set called a population or universe.

Sampling distribution - Distribution of a given statistic in the set of all possible samples from a given population or universe.

Sampling plan - A plan designating sample size and acceptance criteria.

Significant - Indicates variance of a result from some hypothetical value by more than can reasonably be attributed to chance.

Six Sigma - Motorola's term to express a process capability producing only 0.002 defects per million units manufactured when the process is centered and stable.

Stability - Condition or state indicating a process is in a state of statistical control.

Standard deviation - A measure of dispersion of a set of values within a distribution. It is usually designated by the Greek letter sigma. The standard deviation of a sample of size n is denoted by the letter S, and is the square root of the sum of the square deviation form the mean divided by n-1. The standard deviation of a finite population of size N, is denoted by the Greek letter σ, and is the square root of the sum of the square deviation form the mean divided by N. The standard deviation of the distribution of a random variable is the square root of the second moment about the mean, and is usually referred to as the population standard deviation and is also represented by sigma, σ.

Statistical control - The condition describing a process from which all assignable causes of variation have been eliminated and only inherent causes remain; evidenced on a control chart by the absence of points beyond the control limits and by the absence of non-random patterns or trends within the control limits. Also referred to as stable and predictable variation.

Statistical Process Control (SPC) - A method using statistical techniques such as control charts to analyze a process or its output so as to take appropriate actions to achieve and maintain a state of control.

Statistic - Any quantity calculated from a sample, such as the mean, standard deviation or range.

Statistics - Refers to the totality of methods used in the collection and analysis of data, and the science of decision-making in the face of uncertainty.

Total Control Methodology (TCM) - A rigorous system of preventive and proactive control with the objective to preserve an understood process perpetually in a state of functional equilibrium, so as to have all its elements working in synergy, maintaining stability, capability and remaining fool-proof of defects.

Under control - See **Statistical control.**

Variable data - Measurements taken on a continuous scale.

Variance - The square of the standard deviation.

Variation - Change in the value of a measured characteristic.

X. Appendix

Appendix

Tables

Normal Distribution Table [Z: 0 to 2.4 0.00-0.04]

Z	0.00	0.01	0.02	0.03	0.04	Z
0	0.50000	0.50399	0.50798	0.51197	0.51595	0
0.1	0.53983	0.54379	0.54776	0.55172	0.55567	0.1
0.2	0.57926	0.58317	0.58706	0.59095	0.59483	0.2
0.3	0.61791	0.62172	0.62551	0.62930	0.63307	0.3
0.4	0.65542	0.65910	0.66276	0.66640	0.67003	0.4
0.5	0.69146	0.69497	0.69847	0.70194	0.70540	0.5
0.6	0.72575	0.72907	0.73237	0.73565	0.73891	0.6
0.7	0.75803	0.76115	0.76424	0.76730	0.77035	0.7
0.8	0.78814	0.79103	0.79389	0.79673	0.79954	0.8
0.9	0.81594	0.81859	0.82121	0.82381	0.82639	0.9
1	0.84134	0.84375	0.84613	0.84849	0.85083	1
1.1	0.86433	0.86650	0.86864	0.87076	0.87285	1.1
1.2	0.88493	0.88686	0.88877	0.89065	0.89251	1.2
1.3	0.90320	0.90490	0.90658	0.90824	0.90988	1.3
1.4	0.91924	0.92073	0.92219	0.92364	0.92605	1.4
1.5	0.93319	0.93448	0.93574	0.93699	0.93822	1.5
1.6	0.94520	0.94630	0.94738	0.94845	0.94950	1.6
1.7	0.95543	0.95637	0.95728	0.95818	0.95907	1.7
1.8	0.96407	0.96485	0.96562	0.96637	0.96711	1.8
1.9	0.97128	0.97193	0.97257	0.97320	0.97381	1.9
2	0.97725	0.97778	0.97831	0.97882	0.97932	2
2.1	0.98214	0.98257	0.98300	0.98341	0.98382	2.1
2.2	0.98610	0.98645	0.98679	0.98713	0.98745	2.2
2.3	0.98928	0.98956	0.98983	0.99010	0.99036	2.3
2.4	0.99180	0.99202	0.99224	0.99245	0.99266	2.4

Normal Distribution Table [Z: 0 to 2.4 0.05-0.09]

Z	0.05	0.06	0.07	0.08	0.09	Z
0	0.51994	0.52392	0.52790	0.53188	0.53586	0
0.1	0.55962	0.56356	0.56749	0.57142	0.57534	0.1
0.2	0.59871	0.60257	0.60642	0.61026	0.61409	0.2
0.3	0.63683	0.64058	0.64431	0.64803	0.65173	0.3
0.4	0.67364	0.67724	0.68082	0.68438	0.68793	0.4
0.5	0.70884	0.71226	0.71566	0.71904	0.72240	0.5
0.6	0.74215	0.74537	0.74857	0.75175	0.75490	0.6
0.7	0.77337	0.77637	0.77935	0.78230	0.78523	0.7
0.8	0.80234	0.80510	0.80785	0.81057	0.81327	0.8
0.9	0.82894	0.83147	0.83397	0.83646	0.83891	0.9
1	0.85314	0.85543	0.85769	0.85993	0.86214	1
1.1	0.87493	0.87697	0.87900	0.88100	0.88297	1.1
1.2	0.89435	0.89616	0.89796	0.89973	0.90147	1.2
1.3	0.91149	0.91308	0.91465	0.91621	0.91773	1.3
1.4	0.92647	0.92785	0.92922	0.93056	0.93189	1.4
1.5	0.93943	0.94062	0.94179	0.94295	0.94408	1.5
1.6	0.95053	0.95154	0.95254	0.95352	0.95448	1.6
1.7	0.95994	0.96080	0.96164	0.96246	0.96327	1.7
1.8	0.96784	0.96856	0.96926	0.96995	0.97062	1.8
1.9	0.97441	0.97500	0.97558	0.97615	0.97670	1.9
2	0.97982	0.98030	0.98077	0.98124	0.98169	2
2.1	0.98422	0.98461	0.98500	0.98537	0.98574	2.1
2.2	0.98778	0.98809	0.98840	0.98870	0.98899	2.2
2.3	0.99061	0.99086	0.99111	0.99134	0.99158	2.3
2.4	0.99286	0.99305	0.99324	0.99343	0.99361	2.4

Normal Distribution Table [Z: 2.5 to 3.9 0.00-0.04]

Z	0.00	0.01	0.02	0.03	0.04	Z
2.5	0.99379	0.99396	0.99413	0.99430	0.99446	2.5
2.6	0.99534	0.99547	0.99560	0.99573	0.99585	2.6
2.7	0.99653	0.99664	0.99674	0.99683	0.99693	2.7
2.8	0.99744	0.99752	0.99760	0.99767	0.99774	2.8
2.9	0.99813	0.99819	0.99825	0.99831	0.99836	2.9
3	0.99865	0.99869	0.99874	0.99878	0.99882	3
3.1	0.99903	0.99906	0.99910	0.99913	0.99916	3.1
3.2	0.99931	0.99934	0.99936	0.99938	0.99940	3.2
3.3	0.99952	0.99953	0.99955	0.99957	0.99958	3.3
3.4	0.99966	0.99968	0.99969	0.99970	0.99971	3.4
3.5	0.99977	0.99978	0.99978	0.99979	0.99980	3.5
3.6	0.99984	0.99985	0.99985	0.99986	0.99986	3.6
3.7	0.99989	0.99990	0.99990	0.99990	0.99991	3.7
3.8	0.99993	0.99993	0.99993	0.99994	0.99994	3.8
3.9	0.99995	0.99995	0.99996	0.99996	0.99996	3.9
Z	0.00	0.01	0.02	0.03	0.04	Z

Normal Distribution Table [Z: 2.5 to 3.9 0.05-0.09]

Z	0.05	0.06	0.07	0.08	0.09	Z
2.5	0.99461	0.99477	0.99492	0.99506	0.99520	2.5
2.6	0.99598	0.99609	0.99621	0.99632	0.99643	2.6
2.7	0.99702	0.99711	0.99720	0.99728	0.99736	2.7
2.8	0.99781	0.99788	0.99795	0.99801	0.99807	2.8
2.9	0.99841	0.99846	0.99851	0.99856	0.99861	2.9
3	0.99886	0.99889	0.99893	0.99897	0.99900	3
3.1	0.99918	0.99921	0.99924	0.99926	0.99929	3.1
3.2	0.99942	0.99944	0.99946	0.99948	0.99950	3.2
3.3	0.99960	0.99961	0.99962	0.99964	0.99965	3.3
3.4	0.99972	0.99973	0.99974	0.99975	0.99976	3.4
3.5	0.99981	0.99981	0.99982	0.99983	0.99983	3.5
3.6	0.99987	0.99987	0.99988	0.99988	0.99989	3.6
3.7	0.99991	0.99992	0.99992	0.99992	0.99992	3.7
3.8	0.99994	0.99994	0.99995	0.99995	0.99995	3.8
3.9	0.99996	0.99996	0.99996	0.99997	0.99997	3.9
Z	0.05	0.06	0.07	0.08	0.09	Z

Unilateral Normal Distribution Table [Z: 0-2.34]

Z	0.00	0.01	0.02	0.03	0.04
0.00	5.00E-01	4.96E-01	4.92E-01	4.88E-01	4.84E-01
0.10	4.60E-01	4.56E-01	4.52E-01	4.48E-01	4.44E-01
0.20	4.21E-01	4.17E-01	4.13E-01	4.09E-01	4.05E-01
0.30	3.82E-01	3.78E-01	3.75E-01	3.71E-01	3.67E-01
0.40	3.45E-01	3.41E-01	3.37E-01	3.34E-01	3.30E-01
0.50	3.09E-01	3.05E-01	3.02E-01	2.98E-01	2.95E-01
0.60	2.74E-01	2.71E-01	2.68E-01	2.64E-01	2.61E-01
0.70	2.42E-01	2.39E-01	2.36E-01	2.33E-01	2.30E-01
0.80	2.12E-01	2.09E-01	2.06E-01	2.03E-01	2.01E-01
0.90	1.84E-01	1.81E-01	1.79E-01	1.76E-01	1.74E-01
1.00	1.59E-01	1.56E-01	1.54E-01	1.52E-01	1.49E-01
1.10	1.36E-01	1.34E-01	1.31E-01	1.29E-01	1.27E-01
1.20	1.15E-01	1.13E-01	1.11E-01	1.09E-01	1.08E-01
1.30	9.68E-02	9.51E-02	9.34E-02	9.18E-02	9.01E-02
1.40	8.08E-02	7.93E-02	7.78E-02	7.64E-02	7.49E-02
1.50	6.68E-02	6.55E-02	6.43E-02	6.30E-02	6.18E-02
1.60	5.48E-02	5.37E-02	5.26E-02	5.16E-02	5.05E-02
1.70	4.46E-02	4.36E-02	4.27E-02	4.18E-02	4.09E-02
1.80	3.59E-02	3.52E-02	3.44E-02	3.36E-02	3.29E-02
1.90	2.87E-02	2.81E-02	2.74E-02	2.68E-02	2.62E-02
2.00	2.28E-02	2.22E-02	2.17E-02	2.12E-02	2.07E-02
2.10	1.79E-02	1.74E-02	1.70E-02	1.66E-02	1.62E-02
2.20	1.39E-02	1.36E-02	1.32E-02	1.29E-02	1.26E-02
2.30	1.07E-02	1.04E-02	1.02E-02	9.90E-03	9.64E-03

Unilateral Normal Distribution Table [Z: 0.05 - 2.39]

Z	0.05	0.06	0.07	0.08	0.09
0.00	4.80E-01	4.76E-01	4.72E-01	4.68E-01	4.64E-01
0.10	4.40E-01	4.36E-01	4.33E-01	4.29E-01	4.25E-01
0.20	4.01E-01	3.97E-01	3.94E-01	3.90E-01	3.86E-01
0.30	3.63E-01	3.59E-01	3.56E-01	3.52E-01	3.48E-01
0.40	3.26E-01	3.23E-01	3.19E-01	3.16E-01	3.12E-01
0.50	2.91E-01	2.88E-01	2.84E-01	2.81E-01	2.78E-01
0.60	2.58E-01	2.55E-01	2.51E-01	2.48E-01	2.45E-01
0.70	2.27E-01	2.24E-01	2.21E-01	2.18E-01	2.15E-01
0.80	1.98E-01	1.95E-01	1.92E-01	1.89E-01	1.87E-01
0.90	1.71E-01	1.69E-01	1.66E-01	1.64E-01	1.61E-01
1.00	1.47E-01	1.45E-01	1.42E-01	1.40E-01	1.38E-01
1.10	1.25E-01	1.23E-01	1.21E-01	1.19E-01	1.17E-01
1.20	1.06E-01	1.04E-01	1.02E-01	1.00E-01	9.85E-02
1.30	8.85E-02	8.69E-02	8.53E-02	8.38E-02	8.23E-02
1.40	7.35E-02	7.21E-02	7.08E-02	6.94E-02	6.81E-02
1.50	6.06E-02	5.94E-02	5.82E-02	5.71E-02	5.59E-02
1.60	4.95E-02	4.85E-02	4.75E-02	4.65E-02	4.55E-02
1.70	4.01E-02	3.92E-02	3.84E-02	3.75E-02	3.67E-02
1.80	3.22E-02	3.14E-02	3.07E-02	3.01E-02	2.94E-02
1.90	2.56E-02	2.50E-02	2.44E-02	2.39E-02	2.33E-02
2.00	2.02E-02	1.97E-02	1.92E-02	1.88E-02	1.83E-02
2.10	1.58E-02	1.54E-02	1.50E-02	1.46E-02	1.43E-02
2.20	1.22E-02	1.19E-02	1.16E-02	1.13E-02	1.10E-02
2.30	9.39E-03	9.14E-03	8.89E-03	8.66E-03	8.42E-03

Unilateral Normal Distribution Table [Z: 2.40-4.64]

Z	0.00	0.01	0.02	0.03	0.04
2.40	8.20E-03	7.98E-03	7.76E-03	7.55E-03	7.34E-03
2.50	6.21E-03	6.04E-03	5.87E-03	5.70E-03	5.54E-03
2.60	4.66E-03	4.53E-03	4.40E-03	4.27E-03	4.15E-03
2.70	3.47E-03	3.36E-03	3.26E-03	3.17E-03	3.07E-03
2.80	2.56E-03	2.48E-03	2.40E-03	2.33E-03	2.26E-03
2.90	1.87E-03	1.81E-03	1.75E-03	1.70E-03	1.64E-03
3.00	1.35E-03	1.31E-03	1.26E-03	1.22E-03	1.18E-03
3.10	9.68E-04	9.35E-04	9.04E-04	8.74E-04	8.45E-04
3.20	6.87E-04	6.64E-04	6.41E-04	6.19E-04	5.98E-04
3.30	4.84E-04	4.67E-04	4.50E-04	4.34E-04	4.19E-04
3.40	3.37E-04	3.25E-04	3.13E-04	3.02E-04	2.91E-04
3.50	2.33E-04	2.24E-04	2.16E-04	2.08E-04	2.00E-04
3.60	1.59E-04	1.53E-04	1.47E-04	1.42E-04	1.36E-04
3.70	1.08E-04	1.04E-04	9.97E-05	9.59E-05	9.21E-05
3.80	7.25E-05	6.96E-05	6.69E-05	6.42E-05	6.17E-05
3.90	4.82E-05	4.63E-05	4.44E-05	4.26E-05	4.09E-05
4.00	3.18E-05	3.05E-05	2.92E-05	2.80E-05	2.68E-05
4.10	2.08E-05	1.99E-05	1.91E-05	1.82E-05	1.75E-05
4.20	1.34E-05	1.29E-05	1.23E-05	1.18E-05	1.13E-05
4.30	8.62E-06	8.24E-06	7.88E-06	7.53E-06	7.20E-06
4.40	5.48E-06	5.23E-06	5.00E-06	4.77E-06	4.56E-06
4.50	3.45E-06	3.29E-06	3.14E-06	3.00E-06	2.86E-06
4.60	2.15E-06	2.05E-06	1.96E-06	1.87E-06	1.78E-06

Unilateral Normal Distribution Table [Z: 2.45-4.69]

Z	0.05	0.06	0.07	0.08	0.09
2.40	7.14E-03	6.95E-03	6.76E-03	6.57E-03	6.39E-03
2.50	5.39E-03	5.23E-03	5.09E-03	4.94E-03	4.80E-03
2.60	4.02E-03	3.91E-03	3.79E-03	3.68E-03	3.57E-03
2.70	2.98E-03	2.89E-03	2.80E-03	2.72E-03	2.64E-03
2.80	2.19E-03	2.12E-03	2.05E-03	1.99E-03	1.93E-03
2.90	1.59E-03	1.54E-03	1.49E-03	1.44E-03	1.40E-03
3.00	1.14E-03	1.11E-03	1.07E-03	1.04E-03	1.00E-03
3.10	8.16E-04	7.89E-04	7.62E-04	7.36E-04	7.11E-04
3.20	5.77E-04	5.57E-04	5.38E-04	5.19E-04	5.01E-04
3.30	4.04E-04	3.90E-04	3.76E-04	3.63E-04	3.50E-04
3.40	2.80E-04	2.70E-04	2.60E-04	2.51E-04	2.42E-04
3.50	1.93E-04	1.86E-04	1.79E-04	1.72E-04	1.66E-04
3.60	1.31E-04	1.26E-04	1.21E-04	1.17E-04	1.12E-04
3.70	8.86E-05	8.51E-05	8.18E-05	7.85E-05	7.55E-05
3.80	5.92E-05	5.68E-05	5.46E-05	5.24E-05	5.03E-05
3.90	3.92E-05	3.76E-05	3.61E-05	3.46E-05	3.32E-05
4.00	2.57E-05	2.47E-05	2.36E-05	2.26E-05	2.17E-05
4.10	1.67E-05	1.60E-05	1.53E-05	1.47E-05	1.40E-05
4.20	1.08E-05	1.03E-05	9.86E-06	9.43E-06	9.01E-06
4.30	6.88E-06	6.57E-06	6.28E-06	6.00E-06	5.73E-06
4.40	4.35E-06	4.16E-06	3.97E-06	3.79E-06	3.62E-06
4.50	2.73E-06	2.60E-06	2.48E-06	2.37E-06	2.26E-06
4.60	1.70E-06	1.62E-06	1.54E-06	1.47E-06	1.40E-06

Unilateral Normal Distribution Table [Z: 4.70-6.94]

Z	0.00	0.01	0.02	0.03	0.04
4.70	1.33E-06	1.27E-06	1.21E-06	1.15E-06	1.10E-06
4.80	8.18E-07	7.79E-07	7.41E-07	7.05E-07	6.71E-07
4.90	4.98E-07	4.73E-07	4.50E-07	4.28E-07	4.07E-07
5.00	3.00E-07	2.85E-07	2.71E-07	2.58E-07	2.45E-07
5.10	1.80E-07	1.71E-07	1.62E-07	1.54E-07	1.46E-07
5.20	1.07E-07	1.01E-07	9.59E-08	9.10E-08	8.63E-08
5.30	6.27E-08	5.95E-08	5.64E-08	5.34E-08	5.06E-08
5.40	3.66E-08	3.47E-08	3.29E-08	3.11E-08	2.95E-08
5.50	2.12E-08	2.01E-08	1.90E-08	1.80E-08	1.70E-08
5.60	1.22E-08	1.16E-08	1.09E-08	1.03E-08	9.78E-09
5.70	6.98E-09	6.60E-09	6.24E-09	5.89E-09	5.57E-09
5.80	3.96E-09	3.74E-09	3.53E-09	3.34E-09	3.15E-09
5.90	2.23E-09	2.11E-09	1.99E-09	1.88E-09	1.77E-09
6.00	1.25E-09	1.18E-09	1.11E-09	1.05E-09	9.88E-10
6.10	6.94E-10	6.54E-10	6.17E-10	5.81E-10	5.48E-10
6.20	3.84E-10	3.61E-10	3.40E-10	3.21E-10	3.02E-10
6.30	2.11E-10	1.98E-10	1.87E-10	1.76E-10	1.66E-10
6.40	1.15E-10	1.08E-10	1.02E-10	9.59E-11	9.02E-11
6.50	6.25E-11	5.88E-11	5.53E-11	5.20E-11	4.89E-11
6.60	3.38E-11	3.18E-11	2.98E-11	2.81E-11	2.64E-11
6.70	1.82E-11	1.71E-11	1.60E-11	1.51E-11	1.42E-11
6.80	9.72E-12	9.13E-12	8.57E-12	8.05E-12	7.56E-12
6.90	5.18E-12	4.86E-12	4.56E-12	4.28E-12	4.02E-12

Unilateral Normal Distribution Table [Z: 4.75-6.99]

Z	0.05	0.06	0.07	0.08	0.09
4.70	1.05E-06	9.96E-07	9.48E-07	9.03E-07	8.59E-07
4.80	6.39E-07	6.08E-07	5.78E-07	5.50E-07	5.23E-07
4.90	3.87E-07	3.68E-07	3.50E-07	3.32E-07	3.16E-07
5.00	2.32E-07	2.21E-07	2.10E-07	1.99E-07	1.89E-07
5.10	1.39E-07	1.31E-07	1.25E-07	1.18E-07	1.12E-07
5.20	8.18E-08	7.76E-08	7.36E-08	6.98E-08	6.62E-08
5.30	4.80E-08	4.55E-08	4.31E-08	4.08E-08	3.87E-08
5.40	2.79E-08	2.64E-08	2.50E-08	2.37E-08	2.24E-08
5.50	1.61E-08	1.53E-08	1.44E-08	1.37E-08	1.29E-08
5.60	9.24E-09	8.74E-09	8.26E-09	7.81E-09	7.39E-09
5.70	5.26E-09	4.97E-09	4.70E-09	4.44E-09	4.19E-09
5.80	2.97E-09	2.81E-09	2.65E-09	2.50E-09	2.36E-09
5.90	1.67E-09	1.58E-09	1.49E-09	1.40E-09	1.32E-09
6.00	9.31E-10	8.78E-10	8.28E-10	7.81E-10	7.36E-10
6.10	5.16E-10	4.87E-10	4.59E-10	4.32E-10	4.07E-10
6.20	2.84E-10	2.68E-10	2.52E-10	2.38E-10	2.24E-10
6.30	1.56E-10	1.47E-10	1.38E-10	1.30E-10	1.22E-10
6.40	8.49E-11	7.98E-11	7.51E-11	7.06E-11	6.65E-11
6.50	4.60E-11	4.32E-11	4.07E-11	3.82E-11	3.59E-11
6.60	2.48E-11	2.33E-11	2.19E-11	2.06E-11	1.93E-11
6.70	1.33E-11	1.25E-11	1.17E-11	1.10E-11	1.04E-11
6.80	7.10E-12	6.66E-12	6.26E-12	5.87E-12	5.52E-12
6.90	3.77E-12	3.54E-12	3.32E-12	3.12E-12	2.93E-12

Unilateral Normal Distribution Table [Z: 7.00-9.34]

Z	0.00	0.01	0.02	0.03	0.04
7.00	2.75E-12	2.58E-12	2.42E-12	2.27E-12	2.13E-12
7.10	1.45E-12	1.36E-12	1.28E-12	1.20E-12	1.12E-12
7.20	7.64E-13	7.16E-13	6.72E-13	6.30E-13	5.90E-13
7.30	4.01E-13	3.76E-13	3.52E-13	3.30E-13	3.09E-13
7.40	2.10E-13	1.96E-13	1.84E-13	1.72E-13	1.62E-13
7.50	1.09E-13	1.02E-13	9.58E-14	8.98E-14	8.41E-14
7.60	5.68E-14	5.32E-14	4.98E-14	4.66E-14	4.37E-14
7.70	2.94E-14	2.76E-14	2.58E-14	2.42E-14	2.26E-14
7.80	1.52E-14	1.42E-14	1.33E-14	1.25E-14	1.17E-14
7.90	7.85E-15	7.35E-15	6.88E-15	6.44E-15	6.02E-15
8.00	4.05E-15	3.79E-15	3.54E-15	3.31E-15	3.10E-15
8.10	2.08E-15	1.95E-15	1.82E-15	1.70E-15	1.59E-15
8.20	1.07E-15	9.99E-16	9.35E-16	8.74E-16	8.18E-16
8.30	5.48E-16	5.12E-16	4.79E-16	4.48E-16	4.19E-16
8.40	2.81E-16	2.62E-16	2.45E-16	2.30E-16	2.15E-16
8.50	1.44E-16	1.34E-16	1.26E-16	1.17E-16	1.10E-16
8.60	7.34E-17	6.87E-17	6.42E-17	6.00E-17	5.61E-17
8.70	3.75E-17	3.51E-17	3.28E-17	3.07E-17	2.87E-17
8.80	1.92E-17	1.79E-17	1.68E-17	1.57E-17	1.47E-17
8.90	9.79E-18	9.16E-18	8.56E-18	8.00E-18	7.48E-18
9.00	5.00E-18	4.68E-18	4.37E-18	4.09E-18	3.82E-18
9.10	2.56E-18	2.39E-18	2.23E-18	2.09E-18	1.95E-18
9.20	1.31E-18	1.22E-18	1.14E-18	1.07E-18	9.98E-19
9.30	6.67E-19	6.24E-19	5.83E-19	5.46E-19	5.10E-19

Unilateral Normal Distribution Table [Z: 7.05-9.39]

Z	0.05	0.06	0.07	0.08	0.09
7.00	2.00E-12	1.87E-12	1.76E-12	1.65E-12	1.55E-12
7.10	1.05E-12	9.88E-13	9.26E-13	8.69E-13	8.15E-13
7.20	5.54E-13	5.19E-13	4.86E-13	4.56E-13	4.28E-13
7.30	2.90E-13	2.72E-13	2.55E-13	2.39E-13	2.24E-13
7.40	1.51E-13	1.42E-13	1.33E-13	1.24E-13	1.17E-13
7.50	7.87E-14	7.38E-14	6.91E-14	6.47E-14	6.06E-14
7.60	4.09E-14	3.83E-14	3.58E-14	3.36E-14	3.14E-14
7.70	2.12E-14	1.98E-14	1.86E-14	1.74E-14	1.63E-14
7.80	1.09E-14	1.02E-14	9.58E-15	8.97E-15	8.39E-15
7.90	5.64E-15	5.28E-15	4.94E-15	4.62E-15	4.32E-15
8.00	2.90E-15	2.72E-15	2.54E-15	2.38E-15	2.22E-15
8.10	1.49E-15	1.40E-15	1.31E-15	1.22E-15	1.14E-15
8.20	7.65E-16	7.16E-16	6.69E-16	6.26E-16	5.86E-16
8.30	3.92E-16	3.67E-16	3.43E-16	3.21E-16	3.00E-16
8.40	2.01E-16	1.88E-16	1.76E-16	1.64E-16	1.54E-16
8.50	1.03E-16	9.60E-17	8.98E-17	8.40E-17	7.85E-17
8.60	5.25E-17	4.91E-17	4.59E-17	4.29E-17	4.01E-17
8.70	2.68E-17	2.51E-17	2.35E-17	2.19E-17	2.05E-17
8.80	1.37E-17	1.28E-17	1.20E-17	1.12E-17	1.05E-17
8.90	7.00E-18	6.54E-18	6.12E-18	5.72E-18	5.35E-18
9.00	3.57E-18	3.34E-18	3.13E-18	2.92E-18	2.73E-18
9.10	1.83E-18	1.71E-18	1.60E-18	1.49E-18	1.40E-18
9.20	9.33E-19	8.73E-19	8.16E-19	7.63E-19	7.14E-19
9.30	4.77E-19	4.46E-19	4.17E-19	3.90E-19	3.65E-19

Unilateral Normal Distribution Table [Z: 9.40-10.04]

Z	0.00	0.01	0.02	0.03	0.04
9.40	3.41E-19	3.19E-19	2.98E-19	2.79E-19	2.61E-19
9.50	1.75E-19	1.63E-19	1.53E-19	1.43E-19	1.34E-19
9.60	8.94E-20	8.37E-20	7.82E-20	7.32E-20	6.85E-20
9.70	4.58E-20	4.29E-20	4.01E-20	3.75E-20	3.51E-20
9.80	2.35E-20	2.20E-20	2.06E-20	1.93E-20	1.80E-20
9.90	1.21E-20	1.13E-20	1.06E-20	9.90E-21	9.26E-21
10.00	6.22E-21	5.82E-21	5.44E-21	5.09E-21	4.77E-21

Unilateral Normal Distribution Table [Z: 9.45-10.09]

Z	0.05	0.06	0.07	0.08	0.09
9.40	2.44E-19	2.28E-19	2.14E-19	2.00E-19	1.87E-19
9.50	1.25E-19	1.17E-19	1.09E-19	1.02E-19	9.56E-20
9.60	6.40E-20	5.99E-20	5.60E-20	5.24E-20	4.90E-20
9.70	3.28E-20	3.07E-20	2.87E-20	2.69E-20	2.52E-20
9.80	1.69E-20	1.58E-20	1.48E-20	1.38E-20	1.29E-20
9.90	8.67E-21	8.11E-21	7.59E-21	7.10E-21	6.64E-21
10.00	4.46E-21	4.17E-21	3.91E-21	3.66E-21	3.42E-21

Sigmas Versus PPM [1]

Sigma	0.00	0.01	0.02	0.03	0.04
0.0	1000000	992020	984040	976060	968100
0.1	920340	912420	904480	896560	888660
0.2	841480	833660	825880	818100	810340
0.3	764180	756560	748980	741400	733860
0.4	689160	681800	674480	667200	659940
0.5	617080	610060	603060	596120	589200
0.6	548500	541860	535260	528700	522180
0.7	483940	477700	471520	465400	459300
0.8	423720	417940	412220	406540	400920
0.9	368120	362820	357580	352380	347220
1.0	317320	312500	307740	303020	298340
1.1	271340	267000	262720	258480	254300
1.2	230140	226280	222460	218700	214980
1.3	193600	190200	186840	183520	180240
1.4	161520	158540	155600	152720	149860
1.5	133620	131040	128520	126020	123560
1.6	109600	107400	105240	103100	101000
1.7	89140	87260	85440	83640	81860
1.8	71860	70300	68760	67260	65760
1.9	57440	56140	54860	53600	52380
2.0	45500	44440	43380	42360	41360
2.1	35720	34860	34000	33180	32360
2.2	27800	27100	26420	25740	25100

Sigmas Versus PPM [2]

Sigma	0.05	0.06	0.07	0.08	0.09
0.0	960120	952160	944200	936240	928280
0.1	880760	872880	865020	857160	849320
0.2	802580	794860	787160	779480	771820
0.3	726340	718840	711380	703940	696540
0.4	652720	645520	638360	631240	624140
0.5	582320	575480	568680	561920	555200
0.6	515700	509260	502860	496500	490200
0.7	453260	447260	441300	435400	429540
0.8	395320	389800	384300	378860	373460
0.9	342120	337060	332060	327080	322180
1.0	293720	289140	284620	280140	275720
1.1	250140	246060	242000	238000	234060
1.2	211300	207680	204080	200540	197060
1.3	177020	173820	170680	167580	164520
1.4	147060	144280	141560	138880	136220
1.5	121140	118760	116420	114100	111840
1.6	98940	96920	94920	92960	91020
1.7	80120	78400	76720	75080	73460
1.8	64320	62880	61480	60100	58760
1.9	51180	50000	48840	47700	46600
2.0	40360	39400	38460	37520	36620
2.1	31560	30780	30000	29260	28520
2.2	24440	23820	23200	22600	22020

Sigmas Versus PPM [3]

Sigma	0.00	0.01	0.02	0.03	0.04
2.3	21440	20880	20340	19806	19284
2.4	16396	15952	15520	15098	14688
2.5	12420	12072	11736	11406	11086
2.6	9322	9054	8792	8538	8290
2.7	6934	6728	6528	6334	6144
2.8	5110	4954	4802	4654	4512
2.9	3732	3614	3500	3390	3282
3.0	2700	2612	2528	2446	2366
3.1	1935	1871	1808	1748	1689
3.2	1374	1327	1282	1238	1195
3.3	967	933	900	869	838
3.4	674	650	626	604	582
3.5	465	448	432	416	400
3.6	318	306	295	284	273
3.7	216	208	199	192	184
3.8	145	139	134	128	123
3.9	96	93	89	85	82
4.0	64	61	58	56	54
4.1	42	40	38	36	35
4.2	27	26	25	24	23
4.3	17.2	16.5	15.8	15.1	14.4
4.4	11.0	10.5	10.0	9.5	9.1
4.5	6.9	6.6	6.3	6.0	5.7

Sigmas Versus PPM [4]

Sigma	0.05	0.06	0.07	0.08	0.09
2.3	18774	18274	17788	17312	16848
2.4	14286	13894	13512	13138	12774
2.5	10772	10468	10170	9880	9598
2.6	8048	7814	7584	7362	7144
2.7	5960	5780	5606	5436	5270
2.8	4372	4236	4104	3976	3852
2.9	3178	3076	2978	2882	2790
3.0	2288	2214	2140	2070	2002
3.1	1633	1578	1524	1473	1423
3.2	1154	1114	1076	1038	1002
3.3	808	780	752	725	699
3.4	561	540	521	502	483
3.5	385	371	357	344	331
3.6	262	252	243	233	225
3.7	177	170	163	157	151
3.8	118	114	109	105	100
3.9	78	75	72	69	66
4.0	51	49	47	45	43
4.1	33	32	31	29	28
4.2	22	21	20	19	18
4.3	13.8	13.1	12.6	12.0	11.5
4.4	8.7	8.3	7.9	7.6	7.2
4.5	5.5	5.2	5.0	4.7	4.5

Sigmas Versus PPM [5]

Sigma	0.00	0.01	0.02	0.03	0.04
4.6	4.3	4.1	3.9	3.7	3.6
4.7	2.67	2.54	2.42	2.31	2.20
4.8	1.64	1.56	1.48	1.41	1.34
4.9	1.00	0.95	0.90	0.86	0.81
5.0	0.600	0.571	0.542	0.515	0.489
5.1	0.359	0.341	0.324	0.307	0.292
5.2	0.213	0.202	0.192	0.182	0.173
5.3	0.125	0.119	0.113	0.107	0.101
5.4	0.073	0.069	0.066	0.062	0.059
5.5	0.042	0.040	0.038	0.036	0.034
5.6	0.0244	0.0231	0.0219	0.0207	0.0196
5.7	0.0140	0.0132	0.0125	0.0118	0.0111
5.8	0.0079	0.0075	0.0071	0.0067	0.0063
5.9	0.0045	0.0042	0.0040	0.0037	0.0035
6.0	0.00250	0.00235	0.00222	0.00209	0.00198
Sigma	0.00	0.01	0.02	0.03	0.04

Sigmas Versus PPM [6]

Sigma	0.05	0.06	0.07	0.08	0.09
4.6	3.4	3.2	3.1	2.9	2.8
4.7	2.09	1.99	1.90	1.81	1.72
4.8	1.28	1.22	1.16	1.10	1.05
4.9	0.77	0.74	0.70	0.66	0.63
5.0	0.465	0.442	0.419	0.398	0.378
5.1	0.277	0.263	0.249	0.237	0.225
5.2	0.164	0.155	0.147	0.140	0.132
5.3	0.096	0.091	0.086	0.082	0.077
5.4	0.056	0.053	0.050	0.047	0.045
5.5	0.032	0.031	0.029	0.027	0.026
5.6	0.0185	0.0175	0.0165	0.0156	0.0148
5.7	0.0105	0.0099	0.0094	0.0089	0.0084
5.8	0.0059	0.0056	0.0053	0.0050	0.0047
5.9	0.0033	0.0032	0.0030	0.0028	0.0026
6.0	0.00186	0.00176	0.00166	0.00156	0.00147
Sigma	0.05	0.06	0.07	0.08	0.09

Bibliography

1. Mikel J. Harry and Reigle Stewart, "Six Sigma Mechanical Design Tolerancing," (Scottsdale: Motorola Inc., 1988), pp. 10-11.

2. David H. Evans, "Statistical Tolerancing: The State of the Art, Part I. Background," Journal of Quality Technology, Vol. 6, No. 4, (October 1975), pp.188-195.

3. David H. Evans, "Statistical Tolerancing: The State of the Art, Part II. Methods for Estimating Moments," Journal of Quality Technology, Vol. 7, No. 1, (January 1975), pp.1-12.

4. David H. Evans, "Statistical Tolerancing: The State of the Art, Part III. Shifts and Drifts," Journal of Quality Technology, Vol. 7, No. 2, (April 1975), pp.72-76.

5. A. Bender, "Benderizing Tolerances - A Simple Practical Probability Method of Handling Tolerances for Limit-Stack-Ups," Graphic Science, (December 1962), pp.17-21.

Index

benchmark, 183, 216, 284, 322
Bender, A., 222
best-in-class, 185, 192-3, 209, 216
binomial distribution, 223-4, 230, 244
binomial population, 223
Black Belts, 265-8
Bossidy, Larry, 270, 337
Burr-Brown Corporation, 302, 324

C

C&E (cause and effect), 82, 338
cause and effect (C&E), 82, 338
central composite designs, 281
champion, 331
characteristic, 186, 194, 200, 221, 224, 242-4, 247-9, 258,
  260-1, 338
characterization, 260, 263
characterization study, 201, 260
characterization, process, 338, 259-61, 276, 289
characterizing, 191, 202, 204, 211, 221, 324
Chartered Semiconductors, 324
charts, control, 281-2
confidence, 283
control charts, 281-2
control, statistical, 200, 243
controlling, 191, 200, 204, 324
coordinator, site, 266-7, 269, 327, 331
cost-benefit analysis, 224
Cp (process potential index), 187, 191, 216, 217-9, 242-3,
  259, 316, 322, 325

Q

R

*Do you have any comments,
compliments, or corrections
that you'd like to share with
the author?*

Write

Mario Perez-Wilson
c/o ASC Press
P.O. Box 1176
Scottsdale, Arizona 85252
mario@mpcps.com

Advanced Systems Consultants
P.O. Box 1176
Scottsdale, AZ 85252
Tel: (480) 423-0081
Fax: (480) 423-8217
Email: asc@mpcps.com

Order Form

Six Sigma - Understanding the Concept, Implications and Challenges

List Price: US$88 plus $10 S&H, add $5 for each additional book.
Quantity Discount: 10-99 books - 10% discount, 100-more books - 20% discount. Sales Tax: Arizona residents add 7.1% sales tax.

Quantity:

Total Amount is US$:

Customer Information

Name:

Title:

Company:

Address:

City: State: Zip:

Phone: Fax:

Email:

Payment Method

☐ Check Enclosed   ☐ VISA   ☐ MasterCard   ☐ AMEX

Credit Card#:

Exp. Date: